P9-BYY-222

feathers

feathers

Photography by David Cavagnaro and Frans Lanting

Text by David Cavagnaro

Foreword by Roger Tory Peterson

 Graphic Arts Center Publishing Company
Portland, Oregon

Copyright © 1982 by Graphic Arts Center Publishing Company
P.O. Box 10306, Portland, Oregon 97210 • (503) 224-7777

International Standard Book Number: 0-912856-79-3
Library of Congress Catalog Number: 82-82344

Printed in the United States of America

Editorial Direction: Patricia Kollings
Design: Dannelle Pfeiffer
Typesetting: Paul O. Giesey/Adcrafters
Printing: Graphic Arts Center
Binding: Lincoln & Allen Company

table of contents

fOREWORD

It was in the Galápagos, the "Enchanted Isles," that I first met David Cavagnaro. The year was 1964. Scientists from several countries had convened there to dedicate the research station at Academy Bay in honor of Charles Darwin and to engage in a month-long survey of the flora and fauna of the archipelago.

David was still a teen-ager, probably the youngest member of the expedition. As an assistant to the contingent from the California Academy of Sciences, he was already showing the observational skills of a born naturalist. A Galápagos snail *(Naesiotus cavagnaroi)* and several other "new" species that he first collected now carry his name.

The delight young David took in the rich, often exotic array of life forms we were encountering reminded me of my own feelings at his age, when the mere sight of a bird could turn my adolescent listlessness into joyful excitement. The transformation, more emotional than rational, was one my father could never quite understand. Years later perhaps I could have explained it to him in acceptably logical terms: birds are the most colorful, graceful, melodious, and mobile of all known creatures; except for the fishes, they are the most numerous of all vertebrates; they exist in every climate, environment, and geographical corner of the earth except the heart of Antarctica; not surprisingly, they are also the most widely observed and studied of all higher forms of life.

In the course of watching birds, David Cavagnaro's natural sensitivity has inevitably drawn him to the salient feature that makes a bird unique—its feathers. No other living creature possesses these marvels of engineering, but every bird, whether outrageously adorned like the peacock or protectively camouflaged like the wren, has thousands of feathers, each intricately overlaying and interlocked with the next. They give the bird buoyancy, streamlining, aerial maneuverability, thermal regulation, and protection from the elements. The raising or lowering of feathers is also an important component of birds' body language, attracting, repelling, bluffing, expressing alarm, and sending scores of other signals too subtle for human comprehension but instantly recognizable to birds of the same species.

Cavagnaro regards the feather as one of Nature's greatest innovations—"a gift" that has allowed the evolutionary process to create such extravagant possibilities as the global-commuting arctic tern, the effortlessly soaring frigate bird, and the tiny hummingbird whose hovering wings beat a thousand times a minute.

Most "birders," looking at a bird from a distance, reduce its feather-pattern to wing-bars, stripes, and other field marks. If they have a telescope, they may go on to scrutinize it in more detail. Rarely, though, will they take the trouble to examine a discarded feather lying on the beach or the forest floor as Cavagnaro is wont to do. He eschews the telescope, preferring a more intimate look with handglass or macro lens. No bit of down, no insect, no blade of meadow grass is too small or insignificant for his eye to find beauty and meaning and wonder in it.

I cannot now recall whether Cavagnaro was using a camera at the time of the Galápagos experience (though even then he was more of an artist and poet than most of the academic men who participated). In succeeding years, however, I have become aware that he is a photographer of unusual perception. His are not the standard documentary photos one might expect from the trained biologist that he is. They are moving images that convey his deep personal response to what he is seeing.

In this book Cavagnaro includes a number of remarkable pictures by fellow photographer Frans Lanting along with his own. The resulting visual essays are enhanced by short verbal ones in which he explores the origin, diversity, and function of the feather and muses on the deeper lessons it may hold for Man in our time.

—*Roger Tory Peterson*

COURTESY OF AMERICAN MUSEUM OF NATURAL HISTORY

the flicker and the feathered lizard

Sometime before 140 million years ago, a new idea was born into the vertebrate world, an inspiration that blasted open forever the realm of the sky. The feathered lizard Archaeopteryx, *now only a silent messenger in stone, has given us the sole clues from that ancient time of how the miracle of the feather came to be. How much more there would be to tell if only the stone could speak!*

Rainbows grace the world with beauty, appearing unexpectedly out of the darkness of the storm, crowning prince and pauper equally without prejudice or favoritism.

This is the way feathers come to us, floating suddenly out of the sky like jewels from heaven. So also have feathers come to this world as a gift from the far reaches of time.

The fossil record is a narrow window. Through it we view the past as if it were a movie snipped from the reel of life, frame by random frame, and spliced together again by some capricious hand.

The feather — like the flower, which replaced the cone almost without trace of transition — springs full-blown upon the screen of time, unanticipated among the scaly creatures that for eons had impressed the young and forming rocks with their skin casts, footprints, and often giant bones. There is no hint of feathers upon the flaps that carried gliding reptiles for the first time into the perilous but promising sky.

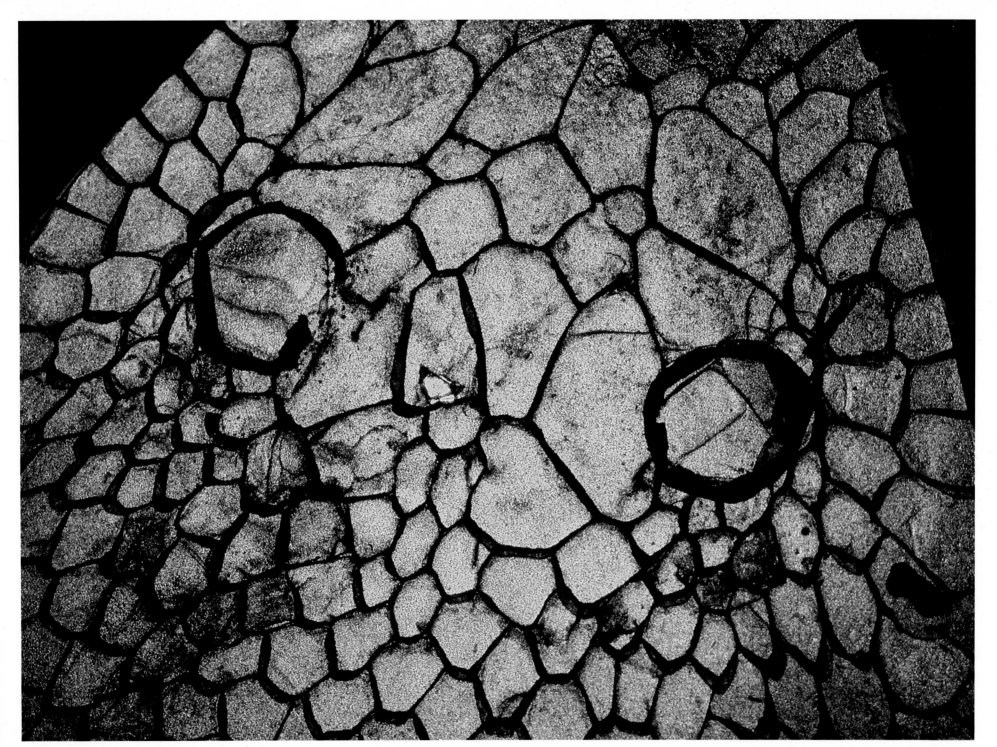

This motion picture of the past would jump from lizard to bird in an abrupt and awesome shift of scene were it not for a single frame that our fanciful editor excerpted from the larger truth. In this one frame we see little Archaeopteryx—a lizard of tooth and claw yet unmistakably also a feathered child of flight—spread out perfectly upon the once-soft mud, as though it had deliberately placed itself there in death to become an exhibit for all time. This silent winged reptile frozen in stone delivers us from scale to feather in an instant. In its promised dominion of the heavens, Archaeopteryx remains one of nature's greatest leaps of the imagination, principal heir to the sky throne.

The feathers that extend from the clawed wings and lizard tail of this haunting protobird, etched there in the rock before us, add as much to the question as to the answer. Are they really only one step in a long but as yet undocumented evolutionary process in which the reptilian scale evolved into the shaft and plume of the feather? Or did evolution speed up just then, passing through some distant time warp so quickly that no series of well-preserved specimens was left behind in the fossil record?

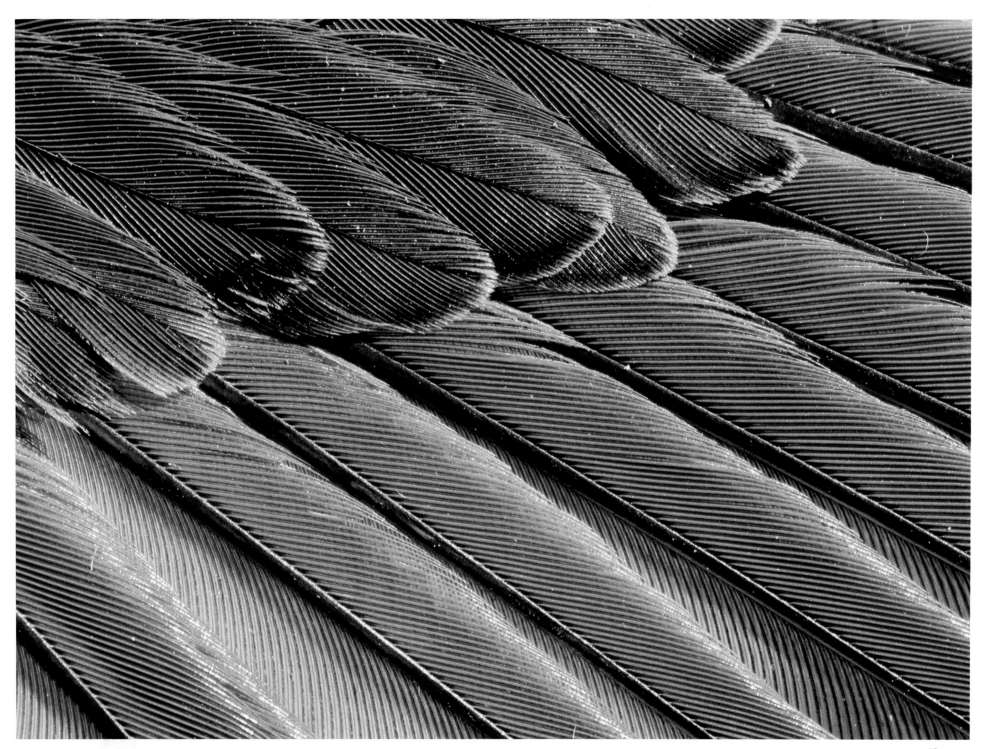

Could it be that, like the evolution of ideas, the evolution of living things contains an element of spontaneity greater even than mutation, one that operates slightly beyond our accepted system of antecedents? Scientists, mathematicians, inventors, musicians, artists, writers, psychics, healers, and mystics have all observed the arrival of creative inspiration from somewhere beyond the materials and knowledge at hand. Might the feather have been an idea, translated by mutation and natural selection from the stuff of a lizard scale, yet born of that same source that gifts the composer with his melodies, the artist with his images, or the poet with his stanzas? Might the feather have been inspired?

As a creation, the feather held more promise than most ideas that have arisen on this earth. Feathers insulate, waterproof, camouflage, and alarm: they adorn, court, attract, and repel. Most glorious of all they can float through the heavens with the lightness of passive thistledown yet be driven toward incredible achievements by that passion for action only animals can manifest.

Sometimes it seems that only thought can go where birds cannot. Since mankind first walked into the light of conscious thinking, we have yearned for the freedom that birds have always symbolized. Now at last we too have mastered the air, flying even higher than birds can. Metal forms our "feathers," insulated by alloys that the searing and friction cannot melt, leaving the very planet behind.

And yet we stand warned by the ancient story of Daedalus and his son Icarus, who were imprisoned by King Minos of Crete. Determined to find a means of escape, Daedalus fashioned wings of feathers set in wax. Triumphantly he and his son skimmed through the air toward freedom. But Icarus, lured by excitement and pride in his power of flight, soared ever higher toward the sun. Ignoring the admonitions of his father, he flew so high that the heat of the sun melted the waxen wings and he plunged to his death in the sea.

Perhaps Icarus speaks to us now across the ages, telling us that we are bound to Earth and that if we become oblivious to its laws we will fall. Neither flights of metal nor of imagination can separate us from the reality that we, like the birds and the ancient lizards that came before them, are creatures of the soil. In spirit we may soar forever, but in body we must land.

One winter morning, clear and cold after heavy rains had broken the fierce spell
of a long California drought, I went walking over the frosted hills to feel the crunch
of frozen ground beneath my feet. The winter migrants were in. There were birds
everywhere, singing, soaring, swooping, feeding across the fields in waves that
rolled against the hillside like breakers upon the shore. As I left the meadow, several red-shafted flickers scattered into the oak woods, where we see them all winter.
And then at my feet I found one that had fallen. Nothing remained but the feathers.

They lay scattered where a hungry hawk or owl had left them. The subtle oranges
and browns were luminous in the soft light of dawn and studded with crystals
of frost. They could have been the jewels of a king, but this king was gone, killed by
a swifter warrior.

So what does it prove, this single frame projected through a narrow slit in time, this feathered lizard frozen in stone, and its legacy, this pile of flicker feathers scattered motionless upon the ground? Perhaps only that feathers — for all the grandeur of their diversity, beauty, and design — and the birds themselves that bear them have not mastered that which cannot be mastered by any creature, not even by man. For man and bird alike are only visitors here. When the frosts of winter arrive, like the flicker we will all be gone; and when the warm rains of spring return once more, some new and even more incredible idea will appear — a melody borne upon the wind from the limitless repertoire of possibility.

the RaiNDROP and the Pelican

The mean February gale had finally subsided to a quiet drizzle during the night. By morning the last puffy white shreds of the storm were straggling in from the Pacific, pursuing the front which had moved on eastward toward the Sierra San Pedro Martir of Baja California.

I sat for a long time on the west cliffs of Isla San Martín, watching the slow, steady progress of grey whales heading south. Having begun their ten-thousand-mile annual migration in the Bering Strait, the whales had nearly reached their destination, the immense, protected lagoons of Scammons, San Ignacio, and Magdalena, where they would calve and breed. San Martín is an important navigation point along the coast, and as the whales swung in close for orientation, I tried to imagine their excitement at finding themselves in the home stretch. They spouted rainbows in the light of the rising sun, and in their blowing I could hear the sound of gigantic bellows fanning the very flames of life.

As the whales pushed on southward, their breathing faded into the wave-sounds of the sea. Suddenly I felt chilled and realized that my leather boots were soaked from trudging around the island through tangles of rain-drenched vegetation. I turned to face the morning sun.

At my feet, young grasses and succulent leaves of ice plant glistened with droplets of water. As my eyes explored the wet carpet, a little feather, white against the green, caught my attention. Bending down close, I could see, as through a lens,

the intricate structure of the feather, magnified by the beads of rain left delicately balanced there.

The feather was from the breast of a pelican. Many others, dropped during molting, littered the cliff edge where pelicans haul in to rest and preen. When I had rounded the island earlier, I had noticed a long line of pelicans gliding so low over the water that at times their wing tips nearly touched the waves. Now a group of them had moved in close against the shore and were circling.

Climbing around another bend, I found a better vantage. The pelicans were diving for fish in a quiet embayment, where the choppy water of the open sea flattened out and a school of fish had gathered. Each bird would climb into the air, its huge wings flapping, until it gained enough altitude to survey the water for signs of food. Suddenly it would drop into a dive, beak and neck outstretched, folding its wings back in perfect timing just as it streaked into the water with a resounding splash.

Over and over again the pelicans rose, circled, and dove, a great wheel of birds that conjured images in my mind of ancient pterodactyls pillaging a Jurassic sea. Soon they were joined by an equally large flock of screaming, pirating gulls, until the little bay was nearly whipped into foam from the kicking of webbed feet and the beating of wings.

When the feeding frenzy subsided, many of the pelicans settled on the water to rest, floating quietly among the blue

Twenty-five thousand feathers emerge dry and essentially undamaged each time a pelican streaks into the water in pursuit of fish.

In a tiny raindrop the magic of the feather is revealed: a zipperlike design that allows feathers at once to insulate, waterproof, and sustain flight.

and white ripples of mid-morning. I marveled that they could still be waterproof after such intense splashing and diving. Four pounds of fish a day are required to sustain an adult pelican; add to that one hundred fifty pounds fed to each young bird before it is fledged, a sizable loss to theft by the gulls, a certain frequency of misses, and the total number of dives a pelican makes during a year reaches a very high number indeed.

I thought again of that delicate little body feather I had seen earlier in the morning, apparently still as good as new after a year's service at sea. Through the magnifying drops of rain I could see the filaments, or barbs, that make up the vanes on either side of the quill. Where the barbs had separated, I could even see the fine barbules that lined the sides of each barb. The barbules are equipped with microscopic hooks, which lock into each other in much the same way as the two sides of a zipper fit together. It is this remarkable piece of engineering that allows a bird to return its feathers quickly to functional condition after rough treatment. With a little oiling and preening, each feather is zipped back together again, its ability to insulate and waterproof fully restored.

In flight, a bird's life depends upon its feathers. Large birds may have as many as 25,000, each of which contributes to the streamlining of its body and each of which must from time to time be preened and kept in good condition. But none are more important in the air than the strong, durable flight feathers of the wings and tail. One large, primary flight feather may consist of a thousand barbs and a million barbules. Each tiny component within a feather, each feather on a wing, each bone and muscle that lies beneath, all work together in an aerodynamic design the efficiency and versatility of which are still the envy of the best aeronautical engineers.

I let my eyes relax; the undulating blue-and-white abstractions of rippling water carried me back along time to that thin slice the fossil record has revealed to us.

The pelican has had a long history beside the constantly changing shoreline of western North America. Giant wing-propelled divers in the pelican order lived along this coast 28 million years ago; up to six feet in length, they were the largest swimming birds known. Supreme gliders lived here also, huge pelican-like fishermen with toothed notches along the sides of the bill and wing spans up to 17 feet — nearly three times the size of the brown pelicans bobbing in the bay below me.

The most ancient ancestors of the pelican are known to have existed at the same time the first whales were making their appearance in the oceans of the world. For 40 million years whales and pelicans have paraded together past this coast, form following function in a magnificent pageant of evolutionary adaptation.

And yet the feather itself is at least 100 million years older than either pelicans or whales. The earliest known fossil feather, perfectly preserved in fine-grained limestone, was found in a Bavarian quarry where lithographic stones were being carefully mined. The fossil was identical in every apparent respect to a modern-day feather. Significantly, the vane on one side of the quill was wider than the vane on the other side. This asymmetry is a feature of flight feathers only and would eventually be recognized as certain proof that the owner of that ancient feather could fly.

A month after the feather fossil was found, a complete skeleton of this flying creature was discovered in another quarry nearby. It had a long, reptilian tail and bony teeth set in a lizard skull. Were it not for the clear impression of feathers in the limestone and a wishbone the like of which is found only in modern birds, the fossil skeleton would have been indistinguishable from that of a small dinosaur that lived in Europe during the same period of time.

Thus the first feathered lizard burst upon the scientific

*A nesting grouse blends perfectly with dry leaves on the forest floor, for camouflage —
the art of being invisible while fully exposed —is yet another attribute of feathers.*

world: *Archaeopteryx lithographica*, "ancient-wing of the lithographic stone." The timing of this new fuel for the fires of evolutionary debate could not have been more perfect — Darwin had published *On the Origin of Species* only two years before. It was clearly time for thought itself to enter the same laboratory of mutation and selection that Darwin proposed for the alteration of species.

The waves that *Archaeopteryx* created in the realm of science, however, were minor indeed compared to those created by the advent of the feather in the scaly world of dinosaurs. Concerning how and when the simple scale of a reptile became the complex masterpiece of engineering we see in the feathers of this ancient flying lizard, the fossil record is so far absolutely silent. All we can say with certainty is that sometime before 140 million years ago a new idea was born in the vertebrate world, an inspiration that blasted open once again the realm of the sky.

Insects had been the first to explore flight 100 million years earlier. Then came pterosaurs, flying reptiles with webbed, bat like wings, who were 20 million years or more into the first experiment in vertebrate flight by the time little *Archaeopteryx* lived. Pterosaurs with wingspans up to 25 feet soared over vast inland seas before sudden extinction claimed them, along with the last of the dinosaurs and toothed birds.

Whatever major events of earth history ended these ancient dynasties, they were not great enough to claim the feather, which was clearly an idea whose time had come. Today, birds are one of the largest class of vertebrates, exceeded only by fish. They comprise 8,600 species ranging in size from the condor, with its wing span of ten feet, to the tiny hummingbird. Meanwhile mammals, which evolved on a nearly identical time schedule, have given us only 4,000 present-day species. Throughout these millions of years of change, dramatic enough for birds of flight and mammals of the land to return to the sea as penguins and whales, the basic types of feathers worn by the primordial lizard bird have emerged essentially unchanged.

Still, as birds have experimented with a wild assortment of designs, adapted to fill every conceivable niche, their feathers have also produced a dazzling number of variations upon the original theme. As I sat in the winter sun on Isla San Martín, I remembered a sweltering June day in northern Minnesota when I nearly stepped on a nesting grouse. She flew up and attacked me in a rage, startling me so thoroughly that I fell backward over a log. Even then, once she had settled again on her clutch of eleven eggs, I could hardly see her, so well did her mottled grey and brown plumage blend with the leaves on the forest floor.

Camouflage is the art of being invisible while fully exposed. Birds that live and nest on the ground, those that feed by night and sleep by day, females that guard the nest, and the young of most species can escape the teeth of keen-eyed predators only if they are not seen. Since there is often neither time to escape nor immediate place to hide, they rely on feather patterns and adaptive stillness to offer instant invisibility. I have watched in astonishment as a dozen quail chicks disappeared so thoroughly in the grass at my very feet that I could not find a single one, even after a long search.

Where birds have assumed specialized functions, their feathers have followed suit. Barn owls, for instance, which are nocturnal hunters, are able to catch mice in total darkness by hearing alone; they are aided by facial-feather disks that gather sounds like parabolic reflectors and by sound-deadening feathers that silence their own flight. Nightjars, goat-suckers, and their relatives hunt for insects at dusk or at night, often catching them on the wing; long whiskerlike feathers greatly increase the effective diameter of their gaping, insect-trapping mouths.

Where birds have assumed specialized functions, their feathers have developed a dazzling number of variations upon the original theme. The barn owl, for instance, is able to catch mice in total darkness by its hearing alone; facial-feather disks gather sounds like parabolic reflectors, while sound-deadening wing feathers silence its own flight.

With only a mild stretch of the imagination, emerging pinfeathers could pass for reptile scales even today.

Feathers seem to arise as suddenly on the back of a barnyard chicken as they appeared in the fossil record.

The feathers of totally flightless birds, like the kiwi, ostrich, cassowary, and emu, are used only for thermoregulation and so have lost, for lack of need, the hooked barbules that make normal feathers aerodynamically sound. Their resulting body covering looks and functions remarkably like the fur of mammals. Highly specialized divers such as the penguins, which also no longer fly, have developed a dense covering of hair-like body feathers, which like the fur coat of seals, is well adapted to the frigid waters of Antarctica. On the flipper-wing of a penguin, where long flight feathers ancestrally grew, there now remain only tiny featherlets, which look convincingly like the scales of a fish.

Nature is not wasteful. Form exists only where it is needed; design that is no longer functional and adaptive is soon cast aside. The long history behind the spouting whales and fishing pelicans I watched that day on Isla San Martín is a tapestry of unbelievable beauty, almost simple in its complexity, for nature bases its creations upon a spare number of laws.

When I returned home from the islands of Baja, the winter air was chill. Most of the Rhode Island reds on the farm wore sparkling new garments; their cast-off feathers were strewn all over the barnyard, rimed each morning with delicate borders of frost. One chicken, however, which we had named Cumulus because she exploded every year in a cloud of orange feathers and white down, had just entered a late molt. Half-naked, shivering even in the sun, she stood separate from the rest of the flock as though embarrassed.

I picked her up and stroked the rubbery pinfeathers that were just beginning to grow in again. With only a mild stretch of the imagination, I thought, they could pass for reptile scales even now. As the next week passed, I watched in amazement as a full-sized, perfect feather emerged from each little stub. Feathers seemed to arise as suddenly and magically on the back of this barnyard chicken as they appeared, according to the fossil record, 140 million years ago.

The origin of the feather, like God and the beginning of the universe, still eludes us. Whenever I see a feather on the ground, like the one in Baja covered with drops of rain or even the chicken feather jeweled with frost, I feel privileged to stand for just a moment in the presence of a great question. That feeling is perhaps as satisfying as discovering an answer.

The exact origin of the feather, like that of the universe itself, still eludes us. Whenever we come upon even the humblest feather, we stand in the presence of a great question.

The eye is the most potent focus of attention in the animal kingdom. A peacock's train spread in display may surely exhibit the most lavish array of "eyes" ever to evolve in nature.

the peacock and the palace

When I was a child, my grandparents had on their farm a flock of peafowl, which roosted at night in an enormous live oak beside the old country house. At the first hint of light each morning, we were awakened by deafening operatics from the cocks just outside the bedroom window as they announced the beginning of their daily courtship routine.

Peacocks are a noisy nuisance at close range, especially the one who made himself at home in grandmother's kitchen, stealing food and preening himself for hours in front of the mirror that hung over the laundry sink. But once I beheld the fully spread tail of a displaying peacock, a fascination was kindled that still maintains a hypnotic hold on me.

Now that I have a farm of my own, peacocks have once again become part of my life, though this time the flock is maintained by a neighbor at a more pleasant distance. Every time the faraway morning cry of courtship slips over the hills and down the valley, a chill of excitement runs up my spine. One spring dawn I finally decided to wander over to the neighbor's with my camera to watch again and photograph this drama that had stayed so vividly in my memory since childhood.

The males were just swooping down from the high oaks when I arrived, their long trains stretching behind them like iridescent contrails. One by one, the hens followed.

Each male flew directly to his own specific dance arena, an area about ten feet in diameter that was nearly bare of grass from constant use. After a bit of warming in the sun and preliminary preening, each peacock lifted and spread his tail, announcing the commencement of his display with the usual ear-splitting cry. I counted six peacocks in their respective arenas around the farmyard.

For a long time the hens grazed some distance away with a number of young males. Gradually, however, the whole group began to move in closer. Each time an immature male passed the invisible outer boundary of an arena, the senior male would aggressively chase it away. The presence of the females, on the other hand, would precipitate a dance of the utmost majesty and beauty.

The hens grazed slowly around the edge of the yard, apparently indifferent to the lures aimed in their direction. Yet they were clearly moving from one male to another. I watched carefully to see which male would win their attention, for I had already picked as a subject for my camera the bird I felt was most striking. He was a magnificent creature with an unusual amount of bronze in his markings. Every feather was in mint condition and perfectly placed in the overall symmetry of his tail. I moved in close beside him and waited.

As three hens inched their way nearer, I could sense the muscles tighten in the peacock's body. A palpable tension filled the arena. He began to rotate slowly in a circle, and the sun, catching his feathers at different angles, caused their iridescence to change from bronze to green to blue. Then quickly he would turn around and flash a bold fan-like pattern of white quills, held erect by the strong, upright feathers of his real tail underneath. With his terra-cotta wings swaying rhythmically, he would back right in among the females and then swirl around again and face them, bathing them in the full brilliance of more than a hundred perfectly arranged metallic eyes.

Throughout this elaborate ritual, the hens simply grazed around the edge of the male's arena. A furtive glance in his direction once in a while, however, indicated that they were indeed noticing. Suddenly, he made a rush for one of the hens and uttered a special high-pitched call reserved for this strategic part of the choreography. In one swift and graceful move he cut her out of the group and brought her into the middle of the arena.

With a hen at close range now, the male intensified his dance. Yet, it was not an increase in activity that signaled the change but rather a narrowing of focus. His eyes and his concentration were riveted on the hen with such intensity that even I began to be mesmerized. With his mouth slightly open and his great train spread in meticulous symmetry, he embraced us both totally in an arching shower of shimmering eyes.

Periodically he would vibrate every feather in his tail, quill against quill, varying the frequency in subtle ways until he created a symphony of sounds as beautiful as wind rustling dry leaves in a forest. Each time the hen tried to leave he would gently catch her and guide her with his outstretched lower feathers as though they were a dozen cradling hands. And when he turned full circle, the great feathers would brush us both softly as we stood together in the arena. I was certain that I, too, would be painted with the vivid hues of his rainbow tail.

For nearly five minutes the hen was held captive by this hypnotic ballet, and yet, though he would have fought ruthlessly for dominance with encroaching males, not once did the cock make a single aggressive advance toward the female. His dance was one of ritualized control, in which every movement was superbly subtle and measured. The hen continued to feign indifference, but once in a while she would turn her head for a moment and stare in dazzled rapture, totally immobilized by the spectacle that enveloped her. Just as quickly she would return to pecking at the ground.

Then suddenly, without any preliminary sign that I could detect, the hen swung around and squatted permissively in front of the male. With his great tail still spread, he mounted, grabbed her by the scruff of the neck with his beak, and mated. After a display that had lasted all morning, the final act was over in less than five seconds. He lowered his tail and casually resumed his preening while the female rejoined the flock.

Like many children throughout the ages, I became fascinated by feathers young. Finding peacock feathers during the summer molt on my grandparents' farm — some of them longer than I was tall in those days — was certainly a spectacular beginning. I also remember being given a box of pheasant feathers that someone in the family had been saving for years. Thirty years later, inexplicably, I still have them. Even now, I find it difficult to pass a feather by without picking it up and at least admiring its striking color or design.

With this old interest in feathers rekindled by my morning of photography among the peacocks, I had a sudden inspiration to examine the patterns of feathers on the bodies of other birds, just as they grow. Since few birds are as obliging about intimate observation as my neighbor's peacocks, I decided to ask if I might look through study skins in the Ornithology Department of the California Academy of Sciences. Thus began four of the most absorbing days of my life.

To my delight I discovered that the collection contained

To intensify the spell of courtship, the displaying peacock makes a quick turn and flashes a bold, fanlike pattern of white quills, held erect by his real tail.

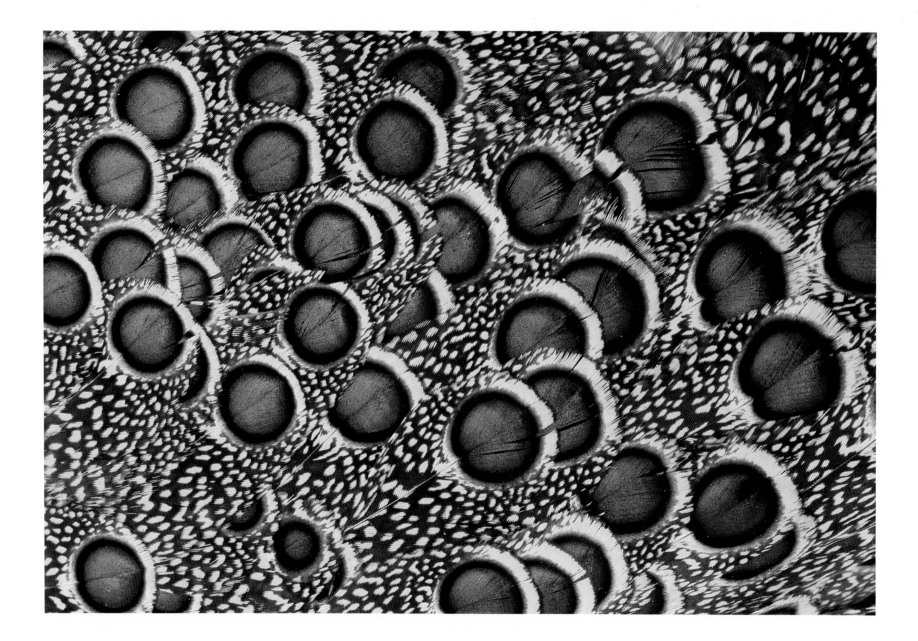

The peacock pheasant may have been the ancestor from whom the peacock
inherited its hypnotic eyes.

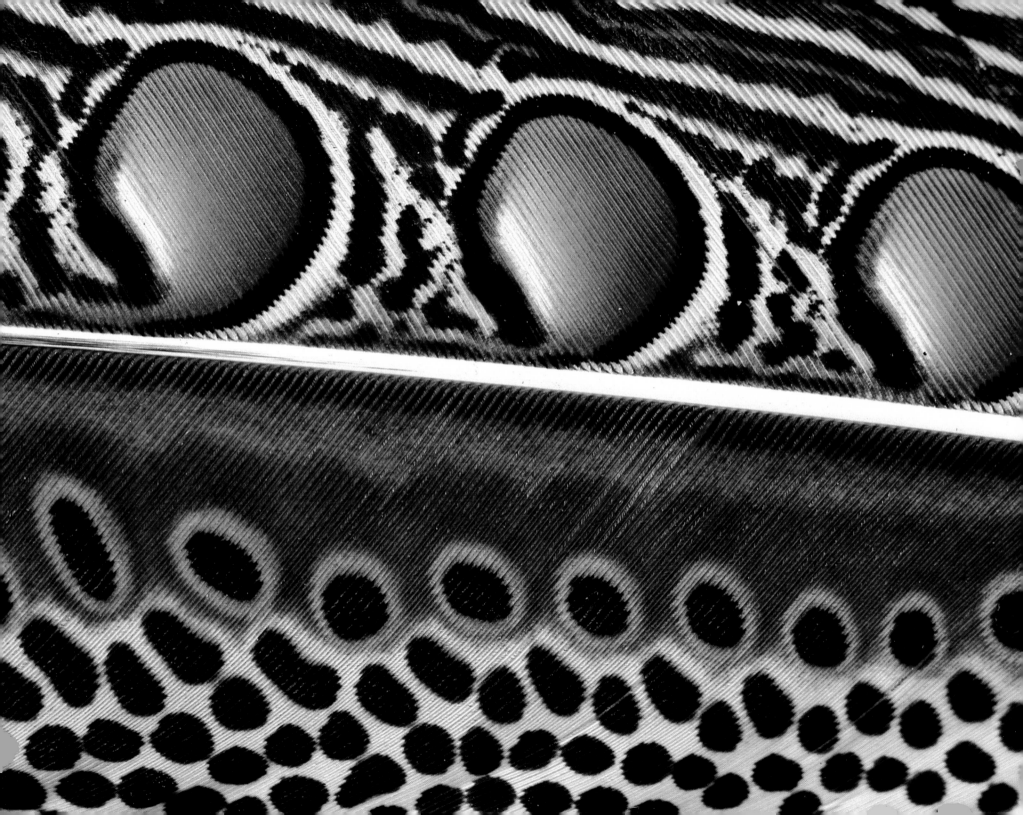

thousands of preserved skins, prepared and stuffed by the skillful hands of dedicated ornithologists a century ago; the feather patterns remained as perfect and as fresh as in life. Tapestries more fantastic than anything I had imagined possible in nature greeted the light as I opened one musty museum cabinet after another. Tucked away in mothballs and darkness for a hundred years in the interest of science, this dazzling display of design reminded me of the collections of robes, headdresses, weavings, feather baskets, and paintings stored in museums of art.

There were red and yellow honeycreepers, whose feathers by the millions once adorned elaborate capes of Hawaiian royalty. Images of tropical forests, trade winds, and Pele, the fierce goddess of fire, flashed across my mind, but then were quickly interrupted by the plumage of gaudy red, yellow, and blue macaws and brilliant turquoise cotingas, used still to decorate ceremonial artifacts along the Brazilian Amazon. Birds of paradise became masks in my mind, worn on the heads of New Guinea highlanders dancing to the light of jungle fires; and red-shafted flickers became ceremonial headbands flashing rhythmically among the redwoods of Northern California. In one cabinet, filled with trogons, I found the famous quetzal, sacred bird of the ancient Mayans; in another lay skins of a bird equally revered by Indian peoples farther north, the eagle. All the lifeless specimens were labeled, appropriately, in the dead syllables of Latin.

The cryptic label on a large case marked *Phasianidae* (Pheasants) left me totally unprepared for the kaleidoscope of Eastern art and history it contained. Native to the highlands of the Himalayas, China, Japan, and Taiwan, pheasants have long been regarded there as sacred. They were domesticated around Asian monastaries centuries before they made their sensational debut among the aristocracy of Europe. All the famous birds were there before me — the elegant copper pheasants of Japan; Reeves pheasants, with tail feathers twice the length of their bodies; the silver, golden, and Lady Amherst pheasants, which could have fallen straight from the silk of ancient Chinese scrolls; and the common ringneck, the world's most popular game bird, whose feathers must adorn the hat of every American outdoorsman. There were the tragopans and eared pheasants of the high mountains of Tibet and northern China, and the shimmering metallic monals, called "oak charcoal chickens" by the people of the Himalayas because their feathers glow like the embers of local cooking fires. The collection also contained the jungle fowl of India and Southeast Asia, a pheasant whose descendant, the common chicken, has through nearly six thousand years of domestication, become the most widely distributed of all birds.

At the bottom of the case, in a large space of its own, I found a skin of the grandest of all pheasants, the peacock, its two dead eyes stuffed with cotton while the eyes of its folded tail stared back at me with all the brilliance of life. There was a majesty in this bird that simply refused to be reduced to a specimen.

In reading about the origin of the peacock's tail, I had discovered that the peafowl's closest relatives are a group of Malaysian birds known as peacock pheasants, whose spotted plumage is richly adorned with iridescent eye spots, or ocelli, on wings, back, and tail. I pulled out a drawer of skins and examined them closely. They reminded me of the guinea fowl whose polka-dot patterns, like the stripes of zebras, so disrupt its familiar shape and features that it can disappear in the dappled shade of the thorn scrub and woodland where it lives. Peacock pheasants, however, inhabit dense tropical forests where light and shadow create such sharp contrasts that even the addition of colorful courtship markings does not alter the effectiveness of their camouflage.

The eye is the most potent focus of attention in the animal

The Argus pheasant, which has developed its immense, eye-studded feathers on its wings rather than its tail, is encumbered almost to the limit of its ability to survive.

kingdom. Predatory animals avert their eyes among their own kind except as a signal of aggression. In some species, colorful ornamentation accentuates the eyes as a featured attraction of nuptial display, while in others, which live where camouflage is required, disruptive designs destroy the eye's circular form. Fish and butterflies have evolved false eyes on their tails so that predators will aim their strikes in the wrong direction; moths and caterpillars, otherwise cryptically marked, flash false eyes for a sudden alarm if disturbed. Even in our own species, the eye has been honored throughout literary history as the window of the soul.

The train of a peacock spread in display must surely exhibit the most lavish array of imitation eyes ever to have evolved in nature. Some scientists have speculated that as peafowl moved from their ancestral forests into more open country and became gregarious for reasons of mutual protection, peahens began selecting as mates those males whose health and vigor was symbolized by their ability to grow the finest nuptial eyes.

There would be a limit, however, to how large ornamented wing and tail feathers could grow without disrupting flight, an ability peafowl would need to retain in order to escape predators in open country. The secretive Argus pheasant of Malaysian jungles, which uses immense, eye-studded wing feathers in a fanned display similar to that of the peacock, presumably has less need to fly in its dense forest habitat and so may have carried wing-feather size about as far as is possible without becoming encumbered beyond the ability to survive. In order to develop the idea of nuptial plumage even further, the peacock utilized perhaps the only feathers available that could grow to such phenomenal length without inhibiting flight: the coverts just above the base of the tail, which have little aerodynamic significance and in other birds are small.

Thus it is theorized that what may be considered the most spectacular male in the animal kingdom gradually evolved from humble, dull-colored ancestors — an idea pushed to its extreme by the ever-growing indifference of peahens to the dazzling dance of eyes. I thought again of the courtship ritual I had watched on the farm next door. While I was so mesmerized by flickering ocelli that I could hardly work my camera, it took what appeared to be the strongest, most perfectly adorned, and most highly controlled peacock some hours to seduce and hypnotize a single female into submission.

As I stared at the study skin in the museum drawer, I remembered the only other peacock skin I had ever seen, in India. It was spread in nearly this same position over its own former body, stuffed with savory dressing rather than cotton, roasted, and served on a gigantic silver platter at the sumptuous table of the Maharaja of Baratpur. Outside on the walls and turrets of the palace, other peacocks strutted to and fro, fitting symbols of royal opulence in this their own native land, where they have lived in semidomestication for thousands of years. The entire meal of black buck, nilgai, and peacock, hunted on the Maharaja's own private game refuge and served at a table set with gold and silver, was in itself a ritual designed to dazzle and impress.

Rituals may have begun as an offering to the gods, a way of communicating with the Great Spirit about the more awesome and frightening aspects of living and dying. However, in the rattling chants of the Indian shaman or the feather-clad dances of the men of New Guinea, it is difficult to separate that part of the human psyche which speaks to God from that part which speaks to its fellow beings. The spires of the great cathedrals may very well reach toward heaven, but inside, the gilded throne of the archbishop is clearly designed to spellbind people rather than God.

Some of our human use of ornamentation accompanies rites

Nuptial plumage is used by many species to mesmerize potential mates in a ritualistic display of intricate designs and brilliant colors. Throughout history our human species has made its own ornamentation from these feathers to accompany rites of passage and courtship, to make offerings to the gods, or to spellbind and control fellow beings.

of passage and courtship. Whether the plumage is worn chiefly by men or by women, and whether it is feathers or automobiles, is a matter of culture. It has been the men of our species, however, who have carried their displays of prowess beyond the personal desire to obtain a mate, control a family group, or corral a harem. Collectively, they have pushed territoriality to such monstrous lengths that this urge, so vital for self-preservation in other species, may well be Man's undoing.

It is the habit of the natural order to test an idea to its limits. Leaders require followers, and together they need territories. Holding a following requires more than a mere display of feathers, no matter how resplendent they may be; so does the defense and, even more, the expansion of a territory. Only a small distance separated a jeweled pulpit from the deadly swords of the Crusades, or the shaman's chants from the battle cry. Neither is it far from the arena of a peacock to the arenas of modern war.

Powerful men of government woo and spellbind appreciative masses by parading their shiny new tools of destruction, rattling their feathers in advertisement of nuclear over-kill. Bombs, however, are not mere symbols as feathers are; these are not false eyes we are being shown. Perhaps, like Icarus, we are about to fly too close to the sun.

Women, the child-bearers, like female birds that wear camouflage to protect their young, are less expendable than men. Perhaps for this reason women have indulged far less than men in historical displays of power. Nevertheless, females can make a difference by their very inaction — peahens by their reluctance to assent, women by their reluctance to dissent.

There is no telling which was the greater slave in this nuptial extravagance, the peacock or the hen. Frederick Douglass, who was once a slave himself, wrote that "the limits of tyrants are prescribed by the endurance of those whom they oppress."

We all dance to an evolutionary drummer, man and bird alike. Perhaps like the peahen, who by her very apathy helped select an extravagance of plumage, the followers of this world, increasingly numbed by ever more potent weapons and greater shows of force, are assisting their leaders in testing to its limits the most dangerous idea life on this planet has ever encountered.

The degree to which we allow ourselves, man or woman, to submit to the tyranny of territorial power and potential annihilation may determine just how close we fly to the scorching sun.

I carefully returned the skins to their drawers, closed the cases, and packed up my camera gear. In spite of the spectral beauty I had seen during these four days at the musuem, the drive back to the farm was not peaceful. How much farther, I kept wondering, can the peacock and the peahen drive each other in this mad race of cause and effect before their experiment ceases to function? At that point, will they be able to alter their course, or will the species perish? Many others have died out before them at the extreme of some evolutionary dead end.

And what about ourselves? It is true that the old principalities of India have been overthrown; the lavish meal I experienced many years ago was only a vestige even then, a mere symbol of yet more palacial excesses earlier. The age of the maharajas has passed, but the thirst for power that drove them to spread their royal tails before the hypnotized peasantry did not die with its passing. That craving has only moved on to larger arenas, where the stakes are far higher. Where will it ultimately lead us?

Now each spring morning I hear a new meaning in the cry of the distant peacocks. They sound more like sirens, as though an alarm were being sent up to Icarus, warning him of his oblivion and his danger.

The extravagant plumage of the peacock may be an idea pushed to its extreme by the ever-growing resistance of peahens to the dazzling dance of eyes. How much farther can they drive each other in this mad race of cause and effect?

the Painter and the Weaver

I can remember as a child finding the broken eggshells of robins lying on the ground beneath their nesting trees. It would have been frightening indeed to find the first such treasure too soon after hearing Chicken Little say, "The sky is falling!" for there are few creations in nature more resembling a chip of sky than the shell of a robin's egg. I was an adult, however, before I had the magical experience of actually looking into a nest. There it seemed that a clear new day was about to be born, so blue were the eggs, and surely the song of the courting robin is beautiful enough to herald the coming of dawn.

The sky was born of the earth, and it has been gradually changed and renewed over time by the quiet fire that burns within the green leaf and by every animal that green things nourish. The earth, in turn, is nurtured by the sky, as the sun draws the water of life from the sea and returns it to the land. As if to symbolize this harmony of earth, air, fire, and water, the robin builds its nest with mud and grass, half bowl, half basket — and then paints its eggs the color of the sky. In searching the universe for the beginning of all that is, we might just as well imagine that this painter, potter, and weaver was the First Artist, who still sings the world into being again each spring.

Robin-egg blue is only one of numerous pastel shades that tint the shells of eggs. In addition, the eggs of many species, especially those laid in open nests or upon the ground, are intricately marked with camouflage patterns of dots, blotches, and lines, which help conceal them from predators when the nests are unattended.

When I was browsing through the study skins in the California Academy of Sciences, I was led also to a large and carefully preserved collection of bird eggs, the markings of which were as amazing to me as the feather patterns I was photographing. The most beautiful in the collection (mostly of North American species), and certainly the most diverse, belonged to the common murre, a seabird abundant along the Pacific Coast. No two eggs were quite alike in color and design.

Over a century ago, during the boom years of San Francisco following the gold rush, entrepreneurs discovered a wealth of murre eggs in the rookeries of the Farallones, some twenty-three miles beyond the Golden Gate. At that time one hundred thousand murres were estimated to nest among several other species on these jagged little islands. Though smaller than a duck, the murre lays a single egg as large as that of a goose and will lay as many as six or eight in succession if they are repeatedly stolen.

Before chicken eggs became a reliable crop in California, murre eggs were highly prized by restaurants and bakeries in San Francisco, where they sometimes brought a dollar a dozen (at a time when flour was only a nickel a pound). "Egg wars" eventually brought the price down to about twenty-six cents a dozen, and after much bitter strife between rival interests one

In the nest of a robin — half bowl, half basket — it would seem that a clear new day is about to be born, so blue are the eggs.

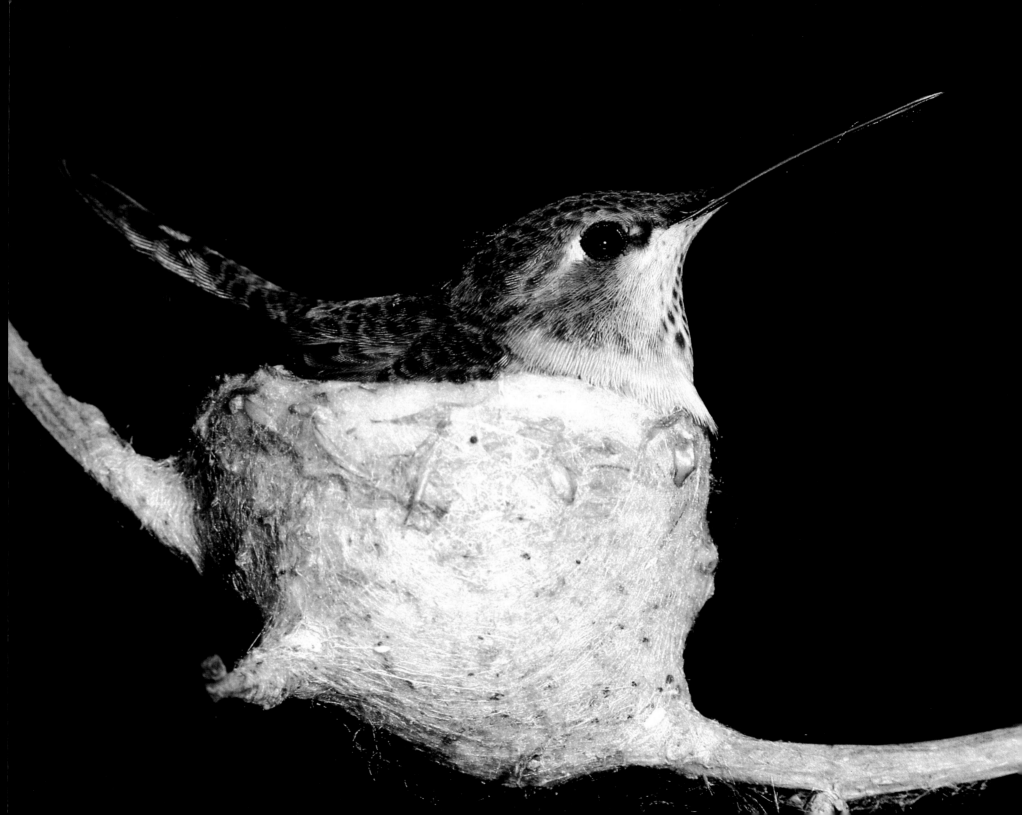

egg company took over management of the resource.

For more than twenty years the harvest continued, during which time as many as two hundred thousand eggs were taken from the rookeries in a single season.

Charles Nordhoff, an author who visited the Farallones in 1874, described the arduous work of the egg collectors: "From fifteen to twenty men are employed during the egging season in collecting and shipping the eggs. They live on the island during that time in rude shanties near the usual landing place. The work is not amusing, for the birds seek out the least accessible places, and the men must follow, climbing often where a goat would almost hesitate. But this is not the worst. The gull sits on her nest and resists the robber who comes for her eggs, and he must take care not to get bitten. The murre remains until her enemy is close upon her; then she rises with a scream which often startles a thousand or two of the birds, who whirl up into the air in a dense mass, scattering filth and guano over the eggers.

"Nor is this all. The gulls, whose season of breeding is soon past, are extravagantly fond of murre eggs; and these rapacious birds follow the egg-gatherers, hover over their heads, and no sooner is a murre's nest uncovered than the bird swoops down, and the egger must be extremely quick, or the gull will snatch the prize from under his nose. So greedy and eager are the gulls that they sometimes even wound the eggers, striking them with their beaks. But if the gull gets an egg, he flies up with it, and, tossing it up, swallows what he can catch, letting the shell and half its contents fall in a shower upon the luckless and disappointed egger below."

Once retrieved from the Farallones, the eggs were unloaded on the San Francisco waterfront for distribution. There was in those wild frontier days at least one man in the city, however, who appreciated these colorful eggs more for art and science than for cakes and omelets. He hung around the dock during the unloading and over a period of time selected the most outstanding eggs from the lot. These comprise the Academy's present collection, safely available to students of nature now, over a hundred years later.

The eggs, sharply tapered so that they resist rolling off the bare rocks where they are laid, come in hues of green, blue, and tan as well as white. Some are bare of markings, or nearly so, but most wear a spattering of black, grey, tan, or brown squiggles and splotches, painted, it would seem, with all the imagination and skill of a modern artist.

Today the bakers of San Francisco use powdered eggs out of cans, and city children know an egg only as a white-shelled, pale-yolked object that comes to the breakfast table via a styrofoam carton; in time they learn that it came originally from one of endless thousands of identical white hens locked up in wire cages—gaunt creatures from which the jungle fowl of India would probably flee if they were ever to cross paths. In San Francisco markets the colorful eggs of the murre are now only a memory.

On the bleak, fog-shrouded, wind-ravaged rocks of the Farallones, the murres and gulls, puffins and cormorants can once again nest in peace. Today these islands are preserved as a refuge where primordial nature is the exclusive patron of the murre's egg-painting art.

The common murre and the robin are far from the only artists among birds. Whatever incredible artistry birds fashion unconsciously with their egg-making apparatus, they more than match consciously with their beaks. The barn swallow sculpts a half-round bracket of grass and mud against the eaves of a building and lines it with snow-white feathers, which it must sometimes look long and hard to find. Cliff swallows may be the greatest avian potters of all, making

Weaving with spiderwebs, the hummingbird creates
a soft, warm nest for its fly-sized young.

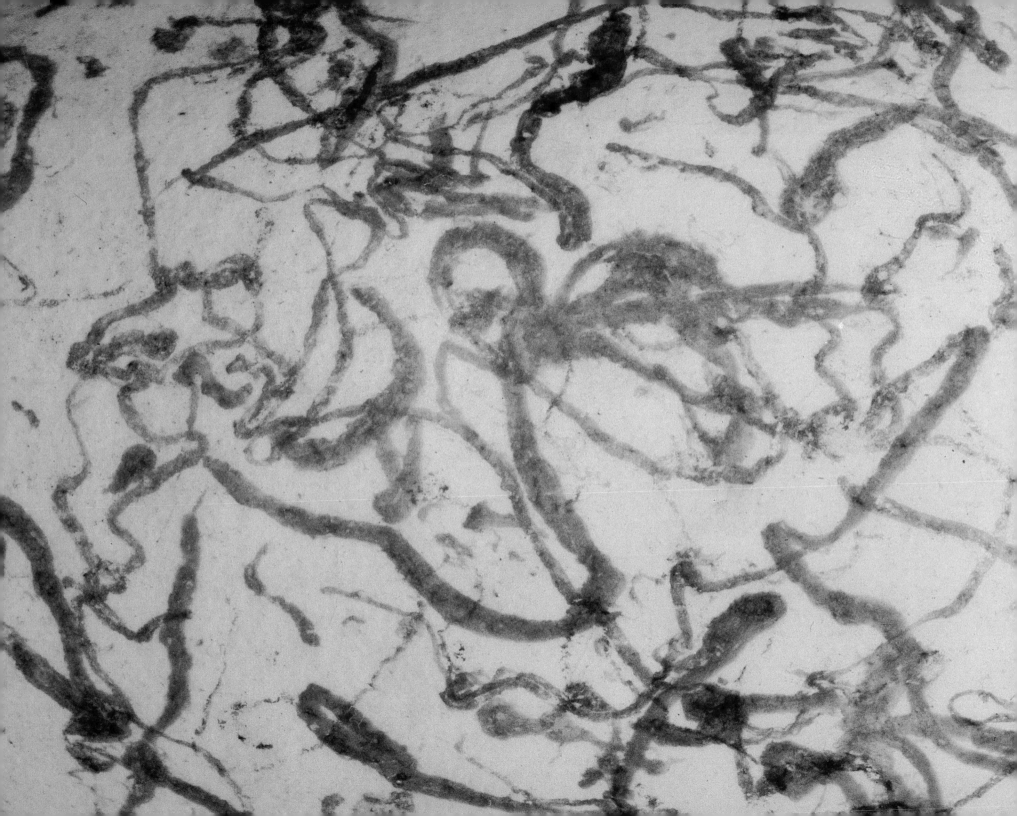

The common murre, like many species of birds, has a highly refined painter's palette in its egg-making apparatus.

hundreds of trips to some nearby wet spot for mud, with which they build, beakful by beakful, whole colonies of beautiful gourd-shaped nests.

The weavers of the bird world, however, have carried the artistry of nest-building to the greatest heights of craftsmanship. Weaving with spider webs, hummingbirds deftly fashion mosses and lichens into miniature baskets that are so well camouflaged that they appear to be part of the branch itself. Then for the comfort and protection of their fly-sized young, they line these nests with the catkin down of the cottonwood and willow, or the fluff of last year's cattails. Very little fiber in nature goes unused as nesting material; branches and sticks by larger birds, twigs by the smaller, often with grass, leaves, shredded strips of bark, feathers, or thistledown added. Where man has increased the variety, nests may incorporate horsehair, string, rubber bands, mattress stuffing, or pieces of the morning paper. Sleeping on the ground out in the woods, I have more than once been awakened by some enterprising nest-builder trying to collect the very hair from my head!

The most extraordinary levels of weaving skill have been attained by the weaverbirds of Africa, close relatives of the ubiquitous house sparrow. Some species build inverted flask-shaped nests of great beauty, suspending them from the outermost twigs of trees, where snakes and other marauders cannot reach. Just as a Pomo Indian basketmaker can recognize the work of another weaver by her unique stitch and design, so also can an ornithologist distinguish the various weaverbirds by the specific stitch each uses in the weaving of its nest, and can even speculate from these patterns something of their evolutionary relationships.

Many weaverbirds are gregarious. The village weaver congregates by the hundreds in single, isolated trees, where the males and females cooperate in building their dangling nests of long fibers nipped and torn by the males from the leaves of palm trees. The Baya weaver of Asia exhibits similar behavior, as many as a hundred pair nesting together in trees around rural villages. Like the village weaver, males of the Baya weaver are polygamous, starting nests and families with several females in succession.

Among all the birds of the world, nowhere has social behavior developed as far as among the social weaverbirds of South Africa. From 100 to 300 pairs work together on the construction of a huge communal apartment house beneath a single thatch roof. The final structure may be 10 feet high and 15 feet in diameter, requiring a sturdy tree for its support.

A totally different path of evolution has been taken by a closely-related bird, whose name has evolved with time almost as much as its behavior. First discovered in Ouidah, a coastal town on the Gulf of Guinea, these birds were soon known as "whidahs," an appellation that through linguistic natural selection eventually became "widow."

All species of widowbirds are both polygamous and parasitic. Some keep harems of up to a dozen hens. The males are adorned with long tail feathers and brightly colored plumage, with which they perform elaborate dances before the females. Some rise 200 to 300 feet into the air, displaying vigorously with their feathers. The paradise widowbird builds an arena four feet in diameter and dances around a single clump of grass, which he deliberately leaves in the center.

Widowbirds, being parasitic, have no need of the complex nests characteristic of their relatives, the weaverbirds. True to natural law, this highly developed weaving skill either atrophied or never developed, for lack of need. Instead, widowbirds lay their eggs in the nests of certain species of waxbills. Since waxbills have pure white eggs, natural selection has eliminated the colors and spots characteristic of all other weaverbird eggs so that the eggs of the widowbird should not be detected among those of its host. To complete the ruse, young widows have developed brightly colored mouths similar to those of their waxbill nestmates.

Nature has always seemed to me to be a living procession of the possible, however bizarre the possible may at times appear. Species move along evolutionary thoroughfares like floats in some gala parade, each one more elaborate than the last. I once read about something called "the totalitarian law of physics," which claimed that anything not forbidden is compulsory. Perhaps biology is ruled by a similar law. Sooner or later, it would seem, every possibility inherent in life and the universe will be attempted. Perhaps nowhere is this principle better illustrated than in the courtship plumage and behavior of birds.

Dancing widowbirds' practice of performing in arenas is shared with the males of many other species, including grouse, lyrebirds, manakins, and as we have seen, the Argus pheasant and the peacock. Of all birds, however, the male bowerbirds of Australia and New Guinea have carried this idea to the greatest extreme, diverting their weaving skills away from nest-building entirely and perfecting them instead in the fine art of arena construction and interior decorating.

As with weaverbirds in their nest-building or pheasants in the development of their plumage, bowerbirds show an evolutionary progression among the various species in the group, their behavior ranging from primitively simple to advanced and complex. While catbirds build no courtship structures at all, the toothbilled bowerbird clears a stage three to five feet in diameter on the forest floor and decorates it with fresh leaves, which he frequently replaces as they wilt; then he sings profusely in and about this area, calling for a mate.

The golden-crested bowerbird is a more advanced stage-maker, who lays a mat of fern fronds on the floor of his arena and surrounds it with neat piles of snail shells, beetle wings, and other treasures of the forest. He even hangs strands of bamboo and fern leaves like a curtain from surrounding vines, replacing and upgrading these decorations daily throughout the breeding season.

Five other species of bowerbirds are called maypole-builders. Using twigs and sticks, the little nine-inch golden bowerbird of northern Australia has been known to build thatch playhouses nine feet tall around a central tree trunk. The "gardeners" of New Guinea construct similar roofed bowers four to six feet tall, the floors of which they carefully plant with lawns of moss that continue to grow in the constant dampness of the rain forest. A rich decor of fern fronds, snail shells, flowers, and piles of brightly colored berries is kept fresh and in order about the floor and walls of the arena.

The avenue-builders have developed the most advanced bower-building behavior. They first pave a four-foot clearing with a deep carpet of twigs. In the center they construct two upright, parallel walls of sticks, carefully woven together, often joined in an arborlike arch at the top, and placed just far enough apart to allow the bird to pass between. This whole arena is decorated lavishly with pebbles, berries, shells, flowers, leaves, and bones.

Both the satin and the spotted bowerbirds of Australia share an intense dislike for the color red. Any red objects placed near the bower are quickly removed, and green berries that happen to turn red after their addition to the decor are ejected forthwith. The satin bowerbird, itself beautifully purple-sheened and blue-eyed, has a strong propensity for any objects that are blue or yellowish in color and will often go to considerable lengths to procure them.

A. H. Chrisholm, in his book *Bird Wonders of Australia*, relates the plight of housewives living within a mile radius of a satinbird's bower. They collectively lost 42 laundry bags — characteristically blue in that region — and were beginning to accuse their children of thievery before the mystery was

The eggs of the killdeer are intricately marked with camouflage patterns,
which help conceal them from predators when the nest is unattended.

solved. Chrisholm also gives this account of items found at a bower near Sydney:

"Eight blue bags, 10 pieces of blue match-boxes, 1 blue cigarette packet, 1 blue envelope, 1 piece of blue string, 34 pieces of blue glass, 17 blue feathers, 1 blue marble, 1 car-park ticket, white with blue printing, 4 blue chocolate papers, 1 blue invitation card to an 'At Home,' 8 yellowish wood-shavings, 2 pieces of yellowish-green onion-peel, 8 snail-shells, 1 cocoon, 6 cicada-cases, numbers of blue and yellowish-green flowers, and a very large quantity of yellowish-green leaves, chiefly the stiff, serrated leaves of the banksia."

It is the spotted bowerbird, however, that perhaps holds the most notorious reputation for stealing. Missing valuables ranging from coins and false teeth to silver spoons and diamond rings have turned up in neighborhood bowers. These enterprising birds have even been known to purloin the keys from cars that were momentarily left untended. One bower in New South Wales yielded the following articles:

"Twenty-four glass corks, 1 jam-tin lid, 2 roofing screws, 7 nails, 5 pieces of tin foil, 1 piece of galvanized iron about 8 inches long, 13 pieces of variously-colored glass, 1 glass ring from neck of bottle, 2 empty cartridge-cases, 21 seed-pods from various native trees, a few small glossy leaves from the coolibah, together with 91 small bones from sheep and emus."

The spotted bowerbird's love for bones at times seems insatiable. Another bower in this same sheep-raising region contained 1,320 sheep bones. In the cattle country of Queensland, where the predominant bones would be too large for the birds to carry, a bower was choked with 2,500 snail shells instead.

In a further extension of the obsession with interior design, three species are known to paint the inside of their bowers with pigments of their own making! The satinbird mixes charcoal with saliva, stuffs a small wad of chewed bark into its bill as a cork to hold back the flow of liquid, and then with its beak methodically paints each stick on the inside of its arbor. Both spotted and regent bowerbirds prefer green leaves, which they chew into a pigment; the latter species even uses a wad of leaves as a paintbrush. Except for the habit of the Galápagos woodpecker finch of probing for insects with a sharp cactus spine, this is the only tool-using behavior known among birds.

These elaborate museums and art galleries of the bowerbirds would be amazing enough in themselves. (When Charles Darwin visited Australia a century and a half ago, Captain Stokes, commander of H.M.S. *Beagle*, was certain that these strange structures were playhouses built by aboriginal women to amuse their children.) But it is what the birds do with their bizarre collection that is most extraordinary. They are forever decorating and rearranging their *objets d'art*, playing and dancing with them, and tossing them into the air — theatrics that are often apparently unrelated to courtship.

As a final addition to their artistic repertoire, both satin and spotted bowerbirds are among the finest mockers in the world. Chrisholm claims there are cases on record in Australia of the spotted bowerbird's convincingly mimicking "the creaking of branches, the twanging of wires as sheep or emus scramble through fences, the squealing of rabbits, the barking of dogs, the croaking of frogs, the rattling of gravel, the 'whistling' of the wings of the crested pigeon, and the voices of many species of birds." He relates stories of how these birds have baffled people with sounds of cowbells and shouting men after the roundup was over, thunder when there shouldn't have been any, and a motorcycle when it was no longer there.

Judging from the behavior of the primitive catbirds and the slightly more advanced stage-makers, bower-building must initially have evolved to promote and enhance courtship. However, the male satinbird is devoted to his bower well beyond the mating season, amusing himself alone there for hours at a time, and the spotted bowerbird seems even to have institutionalized his bower during the off-season as a town hall for neighborhood meetings.

The antics and rituals of these birds seem to have been extended well beyond the sexual drive that spawned them, this perhaps forcing upon us that nagging old question, what is the origin and function of art? For the bowerbirds seem to be at once architects, decorators, painters, singers, and actors who practice art at least some of the time purely for art's sake.

Might these strange little birds be following in the footsteps of man? Was our own first art perhaps the adornment of body and surroundings for the rituals of courtship? Was it only later, then, in our evolution that we began turning our artistic attentions also toward the gods of heaven and earth? Though most art seems to be in some way the voice of the spirit, there is much we still do not know about how or why we create and perceive beauty. And it is true even now, in our so-called advanced stage of culture, that each year more money is spent on cosmetics and fancy clothes than changes hands in all the galleries and fine art auctions in the world.

How much of this decoration of our bodies still has its roots in genetic behavior and ritual, as unconscious as the painting of a murre's egg or the designing of a bower? Or do we adorn ourselves more as a way of seeing other facets of who we are, or projecting new faces toward the world? If so, can we be certain that we are the only creatures on earth that are consciously aware of beauty, self-image, and inner potential? Will we ever know what went on in the mind of the peacock preening before the mirror on my grandparents' porch, or the satin-bird tidying up his bower for a neighborhood convention? Are we sure that we alone know the meaning of art?

the frigate bird and the cormorant

Silently, its engine off, our small boat sailed into the channel between Isabela and Fernandina islands. The massive Galápagos volcanos were brooding quietly beneath an overcast sky. Chill, heavy air embraced the cold Humbolt Current and its host of penguins, making it hard to believe that only a few miles north of Punta Espinoza we had crossed the equator.

It was late in the day as we approached the point, seeking anchorage in its lee so that we could carry on scientific work there for a few days. Spiny black marine iguanas — "hideous looking creatures," as Charles Darwin first described them to the world — were swimming serpentlike toward shore after an afternoon's grazing in the underwater seaweed pastures of the channel. Climbing clumsily from the water, they joined hundreds of their kind basking on the jagged rocks, each one appearing to be, like the black basalt itself, an extrusion of the great volcano.

The iguanas were soon joined by a number of flightless cormorants paddling back from fishing forays into the food-rich waters of the Humbolt. Like the Galápagos lizards and penguins, and the dusky Darwin's finches that live among them, the cormorants are native children of these islands. Descendants of wayward colonists from the mainland, they and many other unique creatures here have been modified in an accelerated way by the pressures and opportunities of isolation and natural selection. When the cormorants hobbled ashore, they spread their wings to dry in the fashion of their ancestors; but where wings should be, we could see only ragged stubs. These birds once came by air across some 600 miles of open water, but by air they can never leave. They are prisoners now on this rocky island coast.

Above us black, primordial shapes were swirling against the leaden sky. A flock of frigate birds had gathered over the boat, hoping to scavenge for scraps of food. Farther out in the channel, a group of boobies were diving for fish, rising fifty feet or more above the sea and plunging bulletlike into the water with hardly a splash. Now and then a frigate would dart away after a food-laden booby, harassing it with maneuvers of incredible acrobatic skill until the poor victim was forced to regurgitate its fish in order to lighten its load and escape. Then in a single swift turn the frigate would swoop down and snatch the falling fish out of the air with its hooked beak.

With a body of less than four pounds carried on a seven-foot wingspan, the frigate has the greatest wing surface to body weight ratio of any bird. What a contrast these wheeling, gliding aerial acrobats created against the backdrop of stub-winged cormorants, forever grounded on the lava flows of Punta Espinoza.

For a long time we watched the huge black birds hang above us almost motionless, feeling out minute air currents we ourselves would not have been able to detect. In the quietness of that moment, my mind wandered upward and became lost in the miracle of flight. As I tried to understand the majesty of

Masters of the ocean skies, frigate birds may stay aloft for days, yet even they must return to earth to nest and raise their young.

what I saw above me, I began to remember fragments of what I had learned about its evolution.

Feathers serve two primary functions: thermoregulation and flight. The features of *Archaeopteryx* that shine forth from the limestones of Bavaria across 140 million years of time are indistinguishable from the feathers of modern birds. Theories, advanced by some, that feathers initially evolved from scales for reasons of controlling body temperature do not explain the feather's intricate microstructure. In mammals, the only other warm-blooded animals on earth, the scales of reptilian ancestors became hair, a far simpler design that serves the needs of thermoregulation just as well. No, the feather seems clearly born to fly.

We may surmise that the bird's earliest prototypes were small lizards, arboreal relatives of the dinosaurs, which jumped from limb to limb in the forested areas. Gliding lizards, frogs, and squirrels have all evolved in similar habitats in more recent time. Any tendency for scales on the legs of these ancient reptiles to elongate, thus facilitating gliding and cushioning falls, would have an immediate selective advantage. Once this change began to take place, the further advantage to locomotion gained by beating the forelegs in the air would begin to select among random mutations for strong pectoral muscles, along with a wishbone and keeled sternum for their attachment — features unique to birds. This flapping of wings, in turn, would provide the rigorous process through which a true feather — light yet strong and able to restore itself if damaged in flight — could also be selected for.

These few basic changes were the only ones needed to make a bird out of a lizard, and they had all taken place by the time *Archaeopteryx* lived (except for the keel, which likely was present then only as soft cartilage). The changes must have happened swiftly, so swiftly in fact that in sifting through the scant fossils of those times, we have not yet been able to find any remains of the animals that experienced them.

I followed the frigates with my eyes, trying to imagine the many refinements of structure and design they and their ancestors had managed to develop across these 140 million years of evolution. Some facts about the many phenomenal achievements of flight began to reassemble themselves from scattered places in my memory.

While the frigate bird can simply soar on outstretched wings for hours or even days, a robin in flight must beat its wings 600 times a minute, and a hummingbird 1,000 times.

Flying can be extremely energetic work, so it required the development of a skeleton of maximum strength and minimum weight, plus a rapid metabolism and high body temperature, good blood circulation, and a highly efficient system of air sacs for breathing (they extend even into some of the hollow bones).

Birds may fly as fast as a hundred miles an hour. In fact, the peregrine falcon has been clocked (by plane) in a dive at 175 miles per hour. The eyes of birds, particularly those of predators, are perhaps the most highly refined in the natural world, exquisitely tuned to receive the greatest amount of information at the fastest possible speed.

It is for their migrations, however, that we hold birds in greatest awe. Most birds migrate at altitudes between 4,000 and 6,000 feet, but tiny shorebirds have been recorded as high as 20,000 feet. Among land birds, the little bobolink makes the longest journey, traveling 7,000 miles from Argentina to Canada. The Arctic tern commutes halfway around the globe twice a year, spending its summers near the North Pole and then, as winter approaches there, heading south to catch a second summer in the seas of Antarctica. Albatrosses have

*Through the loss of flight, cormorants of the Galápagos have become captives on their islands,
totally dependent for survival upon the continued safety of an isolated environment.*

The intricate structure of shaft and vein serves but one purpose—to make the miracle of bird flight possible. Clearly, the feather was born to fly.

been known to travel 19,000 miles around the world, riding wind currents over the open ocean with hardly a flap of a wing.

It is along the major flyways, however, at the points of concentration where waterfowl gather to rest and feed, that the full splendor of migration can be appreciated. At Tule Lake in Northern California, an essential rest stop on the Pacific Flyway, one million birds may be present at one time. The noise and churning mass of this many birds at once could well be one of the most dazzling wildlife spectacles on earth.

As long as humankind has been in this world, there have been birds to inspire us. So much have we admired their achievements that they have been a part of our mythologies and teaching stories as far back as we can see. And long before that, in the distant reaches of our prehistory, birds entered our collective unconscious, where they soar still in our dreams.

Flying is a universal dream experience, an archetype that has much the same symbolism for all peoples. We often dream of our own achievements. Flying in dreams may also give us a vantage from which we can survey the territory where we have been and, in an almost precognitive sense, the paths we have yet to travel.

For some, dreaming of birds may symbolize a sense of freedom from material ties. In many ancient myths, which no doubt had their origin in the same subconscious realm as dreams, birds represented the soul, spiritual knowledge, or clarity of vision. The eagle especially has always represented the ability of our inner thoughts and feelings to rise above the material world, to reach for the realm of the spirit, to see with farsightedness. And the legendary Phoenix, said by the ancients to rise from its own ashes, is a familiar symbol of either spiritual or material metamorphosis.

When feelings of anxiety rather than elation accompany dream flying, however, the symbolism shifts to warning us about over-idealism or flights of fancy in which we may not have our feet on the ground. It is from this facet of the archetype of flight that the story of Icarus was born.

To actually fly in the living flesh has been a desire of man for a very long time. Then suddenly, more than a million times faster than lizards became birds, our earthbound machines became airborne and took us with them. In less than a century, they have borne us far higher than any bird can fly, far faster than the speed of sound, all the way to the moon. Without us, yet alive with our boundless inventiveness and curiosity, they have probed on to the silent, awesome realms of other planets and the dark infinity beyond.

And yet, I wonder. In spite of all this, have we found the freedom of a frigate bird or an albatross? Though our cameras have visited Jupiter and Saturn, can we say that we have seen what the eagle sees?

The anchor was dropped and the sails were furled in a quiet cove lined with mangroves. After assembling our gear, we loaded the panga and made the short trip to shore.

Immediately we were surrounded by tame and curious creatures, fearless in this isolated land that until recently had not known either mammalian predators or human intrusion. Mockingbirds and finches hopped about our feet, pulling at our shoelaces. Yellow warblers inspected us from the mangroves. Endemic Galápagos hawks hovered just out of reach overhead, landing now and then on old snags nearby. And sea lions basking on the white sand beach rolled over as we approached, gave us a curious look, and then fell back into a peaceful slumber. Going ashore among the creatures of the Galápagos is like waking up in some remote time that had never heard of a species called Man.

We spent the rest of the afternoon with the cormorants on their rocky promontory overlooking the Humbolt Current. It

Birds achieve their most awesome feats in migration, traveling as high as twenty thousand feet and as far as halfway around the world.

The noise and churning of a million snow geese at rest-stops along the Pacific Flyway may well be one of the most dazzling wildlife spectacles on earth.

was breeding season, and pairs were busy courting and nest-building, passing gifts of dried seaweed back and forth, and dancing a strange, slow-motion, serpentine ritual together against the reddening sky of sunset.

As primordial as these birds seemed in this weird setting of lava, sea, and sky, the Galápagos cormorant is a newcomer among flightless birds of the world. The whole flight mechanism of a bird averages 20 to 25 percent of its body weight. An enormous amount of biological energy is needed to sustain the anatomical and physiological features necessary for flying. Anything not constantly selected for in nature tends to fall quickly away. Just as cave-dwelling organisms lose eyesight and pigmentation for lack of need, so also when birds are released from pressures that favor flight, they may very quickly be reduced to flightless form. This process has occurred repeatedly through at least 100 million years of avian evolution, particularly when and where large predators were absent from their terrestrial environment.

The most ancient flightless bird we have record of was *Hesperornis*, a loonlike, foot-propelled diver whose bones were discovered shortly after those of *Archaeopteryx*. As these toothed birds and the last of the giant dinosaurs died out in the face of rapidly changing topography and climate, flightless birds began to develop on land. By 60 million years ago some of these had themselves become fierce predators seven feet tall, filling the role vacated upon the extinction of bipedal carnivorous dinosaurs. Similar giant ground birds occupied predatory niches in South America until about 4 million years ago, when they were gradually replaced by large flesh-eating mammals that invaded from the north across the newly-established Central American land bridge.

During the Ice Age there were giant flightless eagles, vultures and owls. The flightless owl of Cuba stood three feet tall, over twice the size of our present-day great horned owl.

The most extraordinary flightless birds of all time were the moas of New Zealand and the elephantbirds of Madagascar, gigantic grazers that evolved quickly in response to the opportunity created by an absence of herbivorous mammals on those islands. Elephantbirds still lived on Madagascar when humans first arrived 2,000 years ago, and moas coexisted with the first Maoris on New Zealand 1,000 years ago. The largest moas were 10 to 12 feet tall and weighed as much as 520 pounds. A single 20-pound egg had seven times the capacity of an ostrich egg; it could hold 183 eggs of a barnyard chicken.

Though moas and elephantbirds are now extinct, large ground birds still exist today. The fastest runner is the ostrich of South Africa, which once ranged widely throughout most of the Eastern Hemisphere. Cassowaries inhabit the dense jungles of New Guinea and emus are common in the grassy woodlands of Australia. The smaller rheas and tinamous are among the last flightless birds of South America.

Within historic times, flightless birds have largely become extinct at the hand of man, as mariners and colonists began to invade their predator-free island refuges. The first to disappear was the dodo, a strange and totally defenseless flightless pigeon, hunted by sailors for meat on the island of Mauritius in the Indian Ocean.

Those island creatures that man himself has not killed for food his introduced livestock and pets have exterminated instead. Feral pigs ate the last eggs of the dodo, and dogs and cats gone wild make easy prey of flightless rails on many islands. The kekapo, ground parrot of New Zealand, is all but extinct, and the kiwis there are not as common as they used to be. The only reason that flightless cormorants still exist on Punta Espinoza is that the feral cats, dogs, and pigs that have decimated entire populations of animals on other islands of the Galápagos have not yet made their way to this desolate shore.

We do not stand apart from the frigate bird and the cormorant in being vulnerable to sudden change....

The cormorant, like many other island species, could quickly become a victim of its own inheritance if faced with predation. While it is a superb swimmer and underwater fisherman, swift enough to escape sharks at sea, the cormorant must rest and nest on land, where its movements are awkward and slow at best. Through the loss of flight, the species has become totally dependent for its survival upon the continued safety of its isolated island environment.

What about the frigate birds that soar and swoop overhead, as though in mockery of the clumsy cormorants drying their shabby little wings in the wind? Though the frigates may stay aloft for days, feeding and even resting over the open sea, they quickly become waterlogged and drown if they land upon the ocean. And just like the cormorants, they too must return to predator-free shores to rest and raise their young. Thus, like all species of living things, even the magnificent frigate bird, king of the ocean skies, has a link in its life cycle that is vulnerable to sudden change.

There is no judgment in nature. All creatures are treated equally by natural law; they simply live where and how they do because they can. If conditions change beyond their levels of tolerance, they are faced with only three possible choices: adapt, migrate, or die. While all life forms seem wondrously well adapted in their present moment of existence, it is those with the most potential to change that hold the greatest promise for the future.

We ourselves do not stand apart, somehow more secure than the frigate and the cormorant. For all our hopes and dreams of freedom, our flying higher than the clouds and farther than the moon, there could very well be little left of us one day but a pile of scorched feathers and a pool of wax melting in the sun.

The choice is uniquely our own. The eagle that soars among the mountain peaks has been our greatest symbol of farsightedness and freedom. Now this, our national bird, is an endangered species. As conscious beings, we must understand not only how the eagle flies, but also why it falls.

...If we alter the earth faster than life can adapt, we may one day go the way of Icarus, with little left of us but a pile of scorched feathers and a pool of wax melting in the sun.

Eventually, the ocean consumes everything, from feathers to continents, yet in its vast womb something new is always being born.

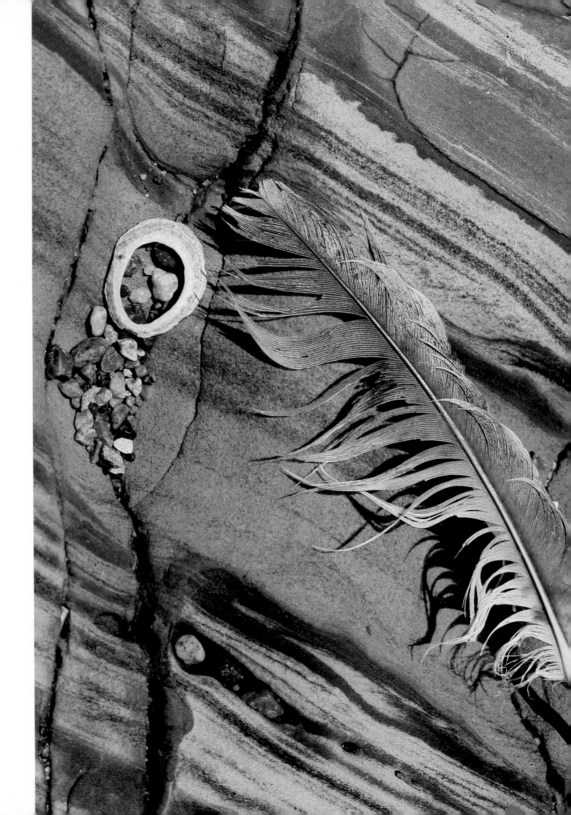

the feather and the stone

The rhythmic roll of breakers against the rocks of Point Lobos rasped at the shoreline like the pulsating radula of a gigantic snail. The tide was low. In protected recesses chitons, limpets, mussels, and clusters of green anemones huddled in resilient defiance of the waves that chewed hungrily at their rocky strongholds.

These rough little creatures of the intertidal world seemed to grip instinct as tightly as they clutched the rocks themselves, choosing just the right spot to nestle in the face of the surf. I pondered the great distance in consciousness that must exist between them and me. I likely could never know, in spite of access to all man's knowledge of the physics of the crashing wave, what these ancient animals of the continent's edge understood in their bodies and their genes from direct experience. And yet, while they knew the colorful, banded Carmelo sandstones only as substrate and personal territory, through some other miracle of consciousness I could perceive these rocks to be among the most beautiful formations along the entire Pacific Coast.

What is it in man that sees beauty, and why? Is it part of the same expanded awareness that allows us to see far back into history and ahead toward the formless future?

I walked higher among the sculptured sandstones, away from the more intense roar of the surf to where the high tide had deposited its many treasures. The rocks were dry now, and little piles of sand, rounded stones, and wave-worn shells lay in Nature's simple, random designs where the last waves left them. On one striped face of stone I found the tattered flight feather of a pelican.

Next to the feather was a worn-down limpet shell, the kind we used to wear as rings on Sunday picnics at the beach when we were kids, and beside the shell an assortment of smooth pebbles had collected in a depression in the sandstone. This little arrangement leapt out at me as though nature had deliberately placed a lesson in my path and then lured me into noticing by creating a pattern I would perceive as beauty. At the time, I photographed this gift from the sea and walked on, my lens attracted next by some petrified ripple pattern and fossilized worm tracks frozen in the uplifted Carmelo sandstones.

There is more to see at the edge of the ocean than the mind can process all at once. Now, four years later, I am studying those photographs in the silence of my studio. I can smell again the salt air and the tossed-up seaweed of Point Lobos, but the only sound I hear is the crashing waves of my own thoughts sifting through the sand grains of time.

These ancient worm tracks and other fossils tell us that the sandstones and conglomerates of the Carmelo formation were laid down near the rim of the continent about 60 million years ago, when modern groups of birds were first evolving. The tiny pebbles left in a dish of sandstone at high tide were plucked from the conglomerates or shredded from the more ancient

Santa Lucia granodiorite, upon which the Carmelo rocks lie. Though their age is less certain, the scant evidence that has survived places their origin before 110 million years ago, at the time of the last dinosaurs, when the only birds on earth still had teeth like their little ancestor, *Archaeopteryx*.

Compared with these aged rocks, the limpet had lived scarcely an instant, a few decades maybe, grazing methodically upon the algae that occupy the rock surfaces of his home range, always returning to his own little hollow in the same habituated way in which we return each night to the snug security of a house. The limpet's calcarious shell might have lasted at most a few years after death, returning gradually to sand and solution at the insistence of the pounding waves.

And the feather? As an idea, the feather is older than the most ancient rocks at Point Lobos by roughly 30 million years. As an individual, functional product of the living flesh, however, this pelican feather cast upon the shore at high tide had served but a one-year term. Its work done, it was shed during the annual molt. Like the pebbles, the shell, and the fossil-rich sandstones, the feather had been cast into the enormous gristmill where stone and water meet, and would in its own time be pulverized and returned to the womb of the sea.

And that, of course, is the most wonderful thing about the ocean: it is a birthplace as well as a place to die. Seeing the ocean only from its edge is like trying to understand a town from walking through its graveyards. Like the heaps of driftwood, rotting seaweed, occasional carcasses, tumbled pebbles, and crumbling shells, even the land itself there is dying, being torn slowly apart by the omniverous waves.

The ocean consumes everything eventually, from feathers to continents, but what it creates anew is of such diversity and scale that we, in our smallness, can hardly perceive its enormous fertility. Limpets will be born here for eons, and after "the age of limpets," some other descendants will live where the limpets had lived before. Minerals dissolved from pelican feather and stone will feed diatoms, plankton, small fish, large fish, and maybe another pelican nesting on a Channel Island south of Point Lobos, an island that in turn will finally disappear into the sea.

If we could speed up the slow-motion pace of continental drift, mountain-building, erosion, and submersion that have sculpted our earth continuously for 3 or 4 billion years, we would see the great oceans of the world moving around the planet like an amoeba, swallowing whole continents, ingesting vast tracts of sediments, forcing gigantic plates of the earth's crust deep into the molten interior of the globe for reforging.

But we would also observe this collective ocean belching forth fiery volcanos, building limestones from coral reefs or the zillions of microscopic animal skeletons in its mineral-rich womb, pressing soft sediments into rigid stone and then, with the help of drifting continents, folding these layers of stone, often miles thick, and hoisting them up into ranges of mountains. What other matriarch on earth has such progenitive powers? The sea is Mother Nature's chief handmaiden in the act of creation.

Change is the one word, if I had to choose just one, that describes the earth and everything that happens upon it. Why is it that we humans resist change so stubbornly when Nature seems to accept it as part of the harmonious order? As routinely as the turn of the seasons, without regret birds drop their feathers each year — even the peacock, for all his apparent egocentricity — and grow new ones.

"One man's burden is another man's treasure," a friend teased me recently when I was finding it painful and difficult to shed thirty-five years of accumulated books, papers, and other no longer needed baggage. How true this has been for all those discarded feathers that have crossed my path over the

One creature's burden is another's treasure. Feathers discarded by their original owners come to us as gifts on wind and wave.

The feather with its million little barbules was not born of success alone, nor was the human consciousness that perceives the feather as a thing of beauty. We have all come from the same terrible magnificence of the crucible of failure.

years; no longer useful to their original owners, each one is a treasure rich in beauty and inspiration to me.

Some I simply enjoy and leave where I find them; others I photograph. An irresistible few find their way into reverent little arrangements on my windowsill at home, just as feathers have entered into the ceremonial rites of all peoples. Some of these have later been given away again at special moments, and the rest eventually feed the clothes moths and carpet beetles that seem to preside over the passage of all sacred objects in time.

I'm looking at some of the photographs now, remembering. There are gull feathers strewn along the beach, some still tangled in an iridescent mosaic of surf foam, some caught in salt grass or flowers, some silhouetted against the orange ball of the setting sun. Here is the body feather of a migrating duck, and I wonder at the enormous distances this delicate, still-perfect object has traveled.

I find a photograph of another pelican feather—a different beach, another time. The memory is clear of that moment when I came upon the sun-dried body of this pelican. Nothing remained above the drifting sand except the tip of one wing and the barbs of a few feathers, reaching for the sky one last time like the sails of a sinking clipper ship.

A Los Angeles manufacturing plant had been dumping DDT wastes into the harbor for several years. Absorbed by diatoms and concentrated along the food web by plankton and fish in the Pacific beyond, enormous overdoses of DDT were accumulating in the pelicans. Hundreds of adult birds were dying, and their breeding success had fallen to nearly zero in the major Channel Island rookeries because the poison in their bodies was causing a fatal thinning of their eggshells.

Sometimes change happens faster than life can adjust to it. This pelican, which had been able instinctively to let go of its feathers in the annual routine of molting, was just as instinc-

tively *un*able to let go of the routine return year after year to nest and feed in the poisoned waters of Southern California. It died at the hands of an unseen monster to which neither its behavior nor its physiology could adapt. Nor could others of its kind. In those years we came very close to losing the chance of ever again finding a pelican feather on a California beach.

Survival for an individual, or even a species, is not a birth-right. There has never on this earth been a guarantee that life would proceed according to "routine." However, what the pelican, the feather, and the stone tell me is that there are basic principles by which the natural order operates that must not be violated if the world is to retain its balance.

Ancient peoples the world over predicted long ago that one day man would step beyond the pale and misuse his knowledge and his power. They have also universally prophesied that such a time would mark the end of an age and that the earth would then receive a great cleansing.

Perhaps ages die in much the same way that species or individuals do. The age of dinosaurs ended abruptly in some mysterious cataclysm that claimed the existence of over 50 percent of all genera of plants and animals living on earth at that time. The twisted rocks of Point Lobos do not speak of a routine and tranquil past.

Life and death, however, are not polar opposites; they are two sides of the same reality, complimentary forces that are interdependent. Conflicts that seem to rage at times between them are merely our perception (or misperception) of their eternal interplay. At its birth, life already contains the seeds of death, and death contains the promise of new life. In the womb of the great ocean, new ideas are always being born, the more so perhaps when there is fresh territory for their experimentation.

If the ancients were correct in foreseeing our future, if this fleeting age of ours is one day ground to sand and pressed

*Survival — for an individual or even
a species — is not a birthright. How many
birds fell fatally to the ground while the
feather was being forged? They still fall. Yet,
just as life contains the seeds of death,
so does death hold the promise of new life.*

into fossils, Nature will only be doing what it has always done: perfecting its imagination. The feather, with its million little barbules, was not born of success alone, nor was the human consciousness that perceives the feather as a thing of beauty. We have all come from the same terrible magnificence of the crucible of failure. How many birds fell fatally to the ground while the feather was being forged? They still fall. And how many ages must pass before we no longer misuse our power?

The death of an age is pregnant with the seeds of fresh possibilities. While warning us of cataclysmic change, the prophecies at the same time encourage us to be gardeners in this vital spring planting, for they claim that our collective consciousness has enough power to alter our destiny and shape the fate of our planet. We will not knowingly destroy that which we come to love and understand.

As we watch wave after wave of human destructiveness sweeping the earth, we feel powerless and frightened. Seeing the body of that dead pelican sinking in the sands of a poisoned sea was like a preview of my own future self, perishing in a quicksand of mass short-sightedness and greed over which, it seems, I have no control. And yet, perhaps I do. Because of the silence that haunted the empty Channel Island rookeries, many voices were raised. They were separate and lonely at first, but soon gained force and swept across the country, reaffirming the laws of Nature that were being violated. Today, DDT is almost totally banned from use in America; this one poison, at least, no longer flows into the beleaguered sea. A few isolated seeds of caring, awakened by a fresh awareness, had grown into a living network for social change.

Every tiny shift in attitude is such a seed, which has the potential of growing into a force that can actually change the way we live. The Carmelo sandstones were laid down one grain at a time, built anew by the sea from the remains of old rocks that had preceded them. In this same persistent way, every thought we hold, every action we take, contains promise for building a new age.

No act of awareness is too small, no moment of attention too short, to be important in this process. We might each pick up a feather, for instance, the next time one falls in our path, and place it on a windowsill as a reminder that beauty and creativity are both ancient and fragile. To touch a single feather with respect is, in essence, to honor all life.

Birds will forever remain for us a reminder of Nature's limitless repertoire of possibility.

afterword

By David Cavagnaro

How I wish I might say to my son as we sit together by the campfire, "I have been an eagle. I have known his mountains and have seen with his eyes the vastness and the majesty of this earth. I have soared through thunderheads, pursuing the setting sun, and have fallen gently earthward as a single feather shed in the depths of a star-filled night. As the feather of an eagle, I have known lightness and strength; I have danced in the sacred dances; I have known the meaning of beauty."

In this and perhaps a hundred other ways I have dreamed the dream of the ages: to fly and be one with the spirit of birds. But I am neither shaman nor mystic; flying with eagles was hardly part of my schooling as a biologist. Now I am simply a farmer who plays with plants and makes photographs as a hobby and who suffers, like most people in our society, from not truly knowing the spirit of *any*thing.

Psychologists who have dissected this malaise of modern times say we are left-brained. They mean that the pragmatic, rational side of the brain has been trained at the nearly total expense of the intuitive right side. More simply stated, we have been programmed to remain on the outside of a thing looking in rather than to be on the inside, in the spirit of a thing, looking out.

In spite of our achievements in material comfort and invention, our lives are often frantic and empty. We yearn to restore the balance within ourselves. Just as water will find its way to the sea, no matter how many times its rivers are dammed, so must our feelings and intuition eventually find expression; so must we also rediscover our essential connection with the natural world.

When I was a child, like most children I had an innate sense of this connection. My backyard world was rich with sounds, smells, textures, and colors; it was peopled with insects, plants, and the many creatures of stream and pond. Interest in these small things of nature led me toward a formal study of biology.

For a while I tried to accept from my college professors that the only sure way to know a butterfly was to dissect its genitalia. The problem I had with this concept, however, was that I already *knew* butterflies. I had raised them from caterpillars, seen them emerge from the chrysalis, watched them unfold their wings in the warm morning sun, and smelled the flowers as they drank their nectar. While other students were thumbing through books, sorting their insect collections to family by counting tarsi under a microscope, I sorted mine instinctively before I even knew what a "family" was. I simply knew them, as certainly as you and I would distinguish cats from dogs, though we might be hard pressed to describe exactly how we tell them apart.

Still, putting names on all those family categories was a satisfying process. Replacing intuitive knowledge with concrete, rational facts was immensely seductive. I was soon deeply bitten by the bug of science and might have lost my childhood sense of knowing forever were it not for one little tool that came into my hands through the wisdom of my family. That tool was a camera.

Ever since, the camera has kept clear an opening between my inner self and the natural world. Through this little window I can still sometimes see with the clarity of a child's eye and achieve at least a limited sense of oneness with the life and elements around me.

When I first focused my lens upon a feather, I felt an immediate surge of kinship. Something ancient deep within me still resonates whenever I photograph them. This book was therefore inevitable, a joyful attempt to capture some of the feelings feathers have aroused in me and to put into words a few of the thoughts they have inspired.

Still, cameras, like typewriters, are by themselves lifeless trinkets. They have no heart, and the more manufacturers and salesmen try to trick us into believing that cameras can see, think, and feel automatically, the less heart we can impart to them through the smokescreen of electronic cybernetics.

The best tools are the simplest. The Olivetti portable I bought twenty years ago has typed five books and thousands of letters while my new electric sits broken in the closet, too costly to fix. My ancient, work-worn Nikkormats, uncomplicated, durable, and totally manual, have taken tens of thousands of photographs, outlasting even some of my first lenses. Everything I use to take pictures except the tripod can be put into one little bag around my waist.

These tools fit my hand and my eye. We know each other now as thoroughly as I once knew the butterflies in my neighborhood, for we have shared life together. They have allowed me some degree of vision and creative expression; perhaps in return I have given them a little bit of soul.

If photographs, like words, are to speak with power, they must flow from the heart. Until I know the eagle with more than the head, my portrait of him will remain as dead as a study skin in a museum. To fully know the eagle, I must fly with him in spirit as well as mind. A true test of this knowledge might be to photograph that dead bird in a museum drawer, or any one of its feathers lying in the grass, and through these symbolic images lift you, the viewer, high up among the crags where the living eagle soars.

This would be a challenge for both of us, existing as we do in relative isolation from the forces that nurture and guide us. Through lopsided training we have all become cripples in a way. No mystic would need a camera to see into the mysteries of this world. Neither do I need a camera nor do you need the pictures I find with it in order to achieve a state of oneness with all that is.

The camera is a crutch that may help us learn to see again. Once we have mastered the art of seeing, we can throw the crutch away. Then at last perhaps we may learn to fly.

By Frans Lanting

One morning recently I found myself sitting beside a turquoise lagoon on a mid-Pacific island, looking at some slides that had just arrived by charter plane from Honolulu. One shot stood out dramatically from the rest — a single Laysan albatross taken during a storm. Its wings were fully stretched, all ten streamlined feet of them, and it was tilting over ready to begin a downwind swoop after reaching the highest point in its meandering flight. Its whole presence radiated grace and quiet strength.

The picture had been made two weeks earlier over the same lagoon whose sunny reflections now provided an impromptu light table. By just changing focus, I could move my eyes back and forth between the celluloid albatross in the mount and the live ones sweeping low over the lagoon. For a long time I played with the alternating images, mesmerized by the marvels of albatross flight — and of photography.

Ever since Edweard Muybridge did his classic photo studies of humans and other animals in motion in the mid-1880s, photography has been used as a valuable tool in expanding our knowledge of birds. High-speed photography has helped unravel some of the mechanics of hummingbird flight; sophisticated flash technology has extended our eyesight into the dark world of owl flight. One need not be a scientist to learn a lot from bird pictures. For example, I had long known intellectually that bird bodies were symmetrical, but it took a picture like that one in my hand, with each black feather on one white wing mirroring a twin on the other wing, to make the abstract fact a living reality. Frozen in motion, the bird on my film also revealed that the albatross flies with its head swiveled around the body axis to maintain a horizontal view of the world while its body, poised vertically on one wing-tip, races downwind at seventy miles an hour. I could never have caught details like that with my eye alone.

That morning by the lagoon, though only a few weeks ago, is already fading into memory; and the stormy day I photographed the albatross seems even more remote. I've seen so many places and so many birds since — an eagle soaring over the snowy peaks of British Columbia; a peregrine falcon plummeting toward its prey along the Big Sur coast in California; a golden plover preening itself on the shoulder of a Hawaiian freeway, making ready for a 2,000-mile non-stop flight to its breeding grounds in Alaska. With each new experience, the island albatross has slipped deeper into the past. Now my photo takes on a new significance. What was once just an interesting study shot has become a precious souvenir. It helps me reach out across time and place to recapture a moment I had to leave behind.

For most people, I think, this is the great appeal of the camera. Our Western culture, so preoccupied with controlling things and events, has not yet learned to harness time. This day, this moment in our lives, will never come back — so we take a picture of it. With each click of the shutter we snatch a slice of the present from the mouth of oblivion. My files, like everyone's, have their share of grabshots, images without soul taken quickly when there wasn't time enough to grow into the place or the creature and thus portray it with feeling. But I made the exposure anyway so that I could preserve *something* of what I had seen, so that I could have something to take home.

The albatross I photographed may be dead by now, or skimming the waves of the Sea of Okhotsk, halfway around the globe, but it left something on my film that was more than just the impression of a moment in its life or in mine. When well done, a wildlife photograph has a universal, almost archetypical quality; it is a moment in the life of Mother Nature herself.

Getting the albatross picture, like most bird-flight photos, involved considerable luck. There is a big gap between clumsy human hands fumbling with awkward equipment and sleek albatross wings driven by a storm wind. Bridging that gap requires the ability to understand and anticipate a bird's movements and to synchronize your own with them. All too often I fall short and end up with only a nondescript blob on the film. But the disappointments are quickly forgotten when unexpectedly in one shot everything comes together, when the hunter becomes the hunted and for a brief moment there is a merger between hands and wings, mind and bird spirit.

If we humans are captivated by photography, we are even more so by flight. It fills our myths and our dreams and our hopes for an interplanetary future — as David Cavagnaro has so eloquently pointed out in this book. The very plane that brought my slides to that Pacific island had a frigate bird painted on its tail. It is as though our species is frustrated not to have happened onto the evolutionary scene at just the moment when wings were being conferred.

Who knows? Perhaps we have been given our oversized minds as a consolation for being grounded. Though we have no wings to lift us up, we have imaginations that will. In spirit we can fly. And for many of us photography is a useful tool for the takeoff.

photographic details

The initials DC denote pictures taken by Cavagnaro; FL, those taken by Lanting. All photos marked "museum specimen" were photographed at the California Academy of Sciences, on Kodachrome 64 film at f22, using 2- to 4-second exposures in the soft, diffused light of a San Francisco fog coming through a window. Nearly all of these were made with a 55mm Micro-Nikkor lens.

PAGE 2: DC. Wing and tail covert area of a male falcated teal, from China. Museum specimen.

PAGE 3: DC. Western gulls landing on Drake's Beach, Point Reyes National Seashore, California. K64, 105mm lens.

PAGE 4: DC. Neck feathers of the Himalayan monal, a species from China that lives at 8,000 to 15,000 feet elevation. Museum specimen.

PAGE 6: DC. Red-shafted flicker breast feathers. K64, 55mm Micro-Nikkor lens f3.5.

PAGE 13: DC. Varied thrush wing backlighted by sun. Highlight metering reduces blue sky to black background. Prismatic refraction of sun through microstructure of these brown feathers causes iridescent colors. K64, 55mm Micro-Nikkor lens, f22.

PAGE 15: DC. The shed skin from the head of a python, backlit by the sun. K64, 55mm Micro-Nikkor lens.

PAGE 17: FL. Snowy egret watching prey in a Santa Cruz, California, lagoon. K64, 400mm lens.

PAGE 19: DC. Wing feathers of a western bluebird, Sonoma County, California. K64, 55mm macro lens.

PAGE 21: DC. Back feathers of the less common green peacock from Southeast Asia. Museum specimen.

PAGE 23: DC. Brown booby, Pearl and Hermes Reef, Leeward Islands, Hawaii. K64 film, 105mm lens at sunrise.

PAGE 25: FL. Frigate bird against the sun, Tern Island, Leeward Islands, Hawaii. K64, wide-angle lens.

PAGE 27: DC. Red-shafted flicker feathers in a winter meadow. K64, tripod shot using 105mm lens and extension tubes, f22.

PAGE 29: DC. Sooty terns at sunset over rookery on Pearl and Hermes Reef, Leeward Islands, Hawaii. K64m, 28mm lens.

PAGE 30: FL. Diving brown pelican, Monterey Bay, California. K64, 400mm lens. Panning with the movement of birds at slow shutter speeds, between 1/15 and 1/60 second, will yield soft motion studies such as this.

PAGE 32: DC. Brown pelican resting in a quiet bay amid rippled reflections of sky, clouds, and cliffs. K64, 105mm lens.

PAGE 33: DC. Water drops on a pelican feather, Isla San Martín, Baja California. K64, 55mm macro lens with extension tubes.

PAGE 35: DC. Back feathers of a gray ruffed grouse, British Columbia. Museum specimen.

PAGE 37: DC. Barn owl portrait taken at the Alexander Lindsay Junior Museum, Walnut Creek, California. K64, 105mm lens.

PAGE 38: FL. Pigeon chick during "porcupine stage," when pinfeathers emerge; Santa Cruz, California. K64, 55mm lens.

PAGE 39: DC. New feathers on the back of a Rhode Island Red chicken. K64, 55mm lens.

PAGE 41: DC. Frosted chicken feather in the barn-yard. K64, 55mm lens.

PAGE 42: DC. Peacock concentrating on a female in his courtship arena (note shade is best for iridescent colors). E400 film, 55mm lens.

PAGE 45: DC. Rear view of a courting peacock, showing the true tail which, when fanned, holds the huge tail converts erect. K64, 105mm lens.

PAGE 46: DC. Body contour feathers of a male gray peacock pheasant from Sikkim, Burma, and northern Thailand. Museum specimen.

PAGE 47: DC. Eyes, or ocelli, on the train of an Indian peacock. Museum specimen.

PAGE 48: DC. Detail from a yard-long Argus pheasant wing feather, backlit on K64 with a 55mm macro lens.

PAGE 51: DC. Neck and breast feathers of a male vulturine guinea fowl from Kenya. Museum specimen.

PAGE 52: DC. Back feathers of a male golden pheasant from central China. Museum specimen.

PAGE 53: DC. Back, wing, and breast plumage of the elegant male quetzal, sacred bird of the Mayans, Central America. Museum specimen.

PAGE 55: DC. Courting. E64, 105mm lens.

PAGE 56: DC. Nest and eggs of the robin. Museum specimen.

PAGE 58: FL. Female hummingbird on a nest woven of spiderwebs, Pinnacles National Monument, California. K64 with flash, 200mm lens.

PAGE 60: FL. Abstract pattern on the shells of common murre eggs from the Farallon Islands. K64, 55mm Micro-Nikkor lens with extension tubes, 4 seconds at f22. Museum specimen.

PAGE 61: FL. Common murres preening each other on the Farallon Islands, California. Elaborate preening rituals among murres seem to strengthen pair bonding. K64, 500mm lens.

PAGE 64: FL. Killdeer eggs in a gravel-bed nest, Trinity Alps, California. Tripod, K64 in overcast light, 105mm lens and extension tubes.

PAGE 65: FL. Killdeer sitting on the same clutch of eggs. This picture was taken while lying flat on the ground after approaching slowly to gain the confidence of the bird. K64, 135mm lens and extension tubes from a distance of 2 feet.

PAGE 68: FL. Flock of frigate birds hovering over a boat in the Galápagos Islands, Ecuador, on a dark, overcast day. K64, 105mm lens.

PAGE 71: FL. Courting flightless cormorant giving its mate a ceremonial gift of seaweed, Punta Espinoza, Galápagos. K64, 105mm lens.

PAGE 72: FL. Galápagos hawk against the sun, Volcan Alcedo. K64, 105mm lens.

PAGE 73: FL. Peacock primary feather detail, backlit on K64 with 55mm Micro-Nikkor lens and extension tubes.

PAGE 75: FL. Marbled godwit landing in a flock of shorebirds, Laguna San Ignacio, Baja California. K64, 400mm lens at ground level. The long, slow belly crawl is the best approach to win the confidence of resting birds.

PAGE 76: FL. Snow geese, Tule Lake, California. K64, 400mm lens.

PAGE 77: FL. Snow geese in evening flight, Tule Lake fall migration. E400, 24mm lens, slow shutter speed in the dim light of evening among twenty thousand birds.

PAGE 79: DC. Flightless cormorant preening at sundown, Punta Espinoza, Galápagos Islands. K64, 105mm lens.

PAGE 81: DC. Gull feather and the midnight sun, Safety Lagoon, Nome, Alaska. E400 film, 55mm Micro-Nikkor lens with extension tubes, aperture wide open.

PAGE 82: DC. Wave-worn brown pelican feather washed ashore on the Carmelo sandstone formation, Point Lobos, California. K64, 55mm lens.

PAGE 85: DC. Gull feather and storm-surf bubbles, Point Reyes National Seashore, California. Old High Speed Ektrachrome, 55mm lens.

PAGE 86: DC. Dead bird fallen among autumn maple leaves, Lake Superior shore, Ontario. K64, 55mm lens on a tripod, long exposure at f22.

PAGE 87: DC. Gull feather detail against the midnight sun near Nome, Alaska. K64, 55mm macro lens with extension tubes, wide open aperture.

PAGE 89: FL. Horsetail shoot sprouting through the wing of a dead cormorant, Año Nuevo Island, California. K64, 55mm lens.

PAGE 91: FL. Snowy egret in flight, Santa Cruz, California. E64, 400mm lens, a motion study at about 1/4 or 1/2 second, panning with the bird.

acknowledgements

We would like to extend our gratitude to the Ornithology Department staff of the California Academy of Sciences for access to collections and answers to frequent questions, and to the personnel of wildlife reserves in the West, especially Klamath Basin, San Francisco Bay, and Hawaiian Islands national wildlife refuges, for making field work possible. We thank also many friends in the Environmental Studies and Marine Studies departments of the University of California Santa Cruz campus, the Santa Cruz Predatory Bird Research Group, and Point Reyes Bird Observatory for inspiration and help in gaining access to places teeming with birds.

Special appreciation is extended to Roger Tory Peterson for checking the manuscript and providing the book with a foreword, and to Les Line, editor of *Audubon* magazine, for publishing "From Scales Descended or of Inspiration Born?" — an essay that spawned this book and is reproduced here (by permission) in new form as "The Flicker and the Feathered Lizard."

Editor Patricia Kollings, an eagle with words, helped many a fledgling phrase get airborne. She has continued, on this their fourth book together, to preen the author's prose and occasionally even his thoughts to fly a little higher.

DAVID CAVAGNARO
SANTA ROSA, CALIFORNIA

FRANS LANTING
SANTA CRUZ, CALIFORNIA